Lost In Church Translation:
Finding Christ In Christianity

Robert E. Buckner, II

Copyright © 2017 Robert E. Buckner, II
Foreword © 2017 Ozzie E. Smith, Jr.

All rights reserved. No part of this publication may be reproduced, distributed, or transmitted in any form or by any means, including photocopying, recording, or other electronic or mechanical methods, without the prior written permission of the publisher, except in the case of brief quotations embodied in critical reviews and certain other noncommercial uses permitted by copyright law.

For more information or request please visit www.RobBuckner.com

Scripture quotations are taken from or paraphrased from the New Revised Standard Version Bible, copyright © 1989 the Division of Christian Education of the National Council of the Churches of Christ in the United States of America. Used by permission.

Library of Congress Cataloging-in-Publication Data has been applied for.

ISBN: 0999309005
ISBN-13: 978-0999309001

Printed in the United States of America

rebEL Faith Publishing, First Edition

DEDICATION

To the faces that allow me to see God daily – Mary, Caleb and Micah
To those who pointed me to God – Cordella, Noble, Linda and Bridget
To the thing that made me believe in God -- LIFE

CONTENTS

	Foreword	i
	Preface	iii
1	It's Complicated	1
2	We Need To Talk: Conversational Prayer	11
3	I'll Have What He's Having: God's Life, His Purpose	23
4	Seeing Things: Vision	31
5	What'll Ya Have: Serving	35
6	The Power of Praise	45
7	Worship As A Witness	53
8	I Got Ten On It: Tithing and Offering	63
9	The Devil Made ME Do It: Sin	69
10	What's Love Got To Do with It: Love	81
11	The Good Life: Salvation	87
12	Life After Benediction	95
	Acknowledgments	101

FOREWORD

Robert Buckner takes a critical look at why it seems that the faith story in over 45,000 denominations has not been created equal. Not unlike historical biblical evidence tells us, the eyes, hands, and voices of humanity when handling God's Word, somehow shape it into their own image. There are varying strands of religion that seem to have nothing in common with the original faith narrative or founders. Buckner contends that this reality becomes confusing to would-be Christians. Not unlike learning in seminary that there are Greek and Hebrew words for which there are no English equivalents, something gets lost in translation. Likewise, each faith community has belief for which there are no Christian equivalents. The "real" of the faith likewise gets diluted from church to church.

This book was inspired by a question stemming from a barbershop dialogue on whether or not the Bible is worth believing given its human origins. Likewise, there is a gut belief that something was lost in both transmission and translation. Buckner examines at least three questions borne out of that debate: "What do we believe?" "Why should we believe?" or "Why bother to believe at all?" The book title suggests that faith is largely lost in translation as it is taught from one church to the other. People come to church with critical life questions, but leave with even more questions, and at times no understanding of God. Buckner does not make a value judgment at the seeming un-level worship field, but explores a plethora of reasons as to why there is a five hundred pound belief question seated in sanctuaries of our times. His discussion goes beyond denominations alone, but to the subtle but huge differences of sanctuary experience. Somehow after Matthew, Mark, Luke, and John, adherents seem to have gotten things twisted, dismissed, ignored, or lost in translation. Buckner begs the question, "What would Jesus join?"

Buckner's use of Church translation as metaphor is well said with poignant analogies and illustrations. He does not attempt to provide the end-all answer, but suggests ways of discipline and balance to undergird faith in an age of fragmented belief and unbelief. Could it be that this issue is a child of post-enlightenment that has birthed such darkness? Buckner dares to suggest that though a reasonable consensus is possible, it is not probable given the limits and capriciousness of human nature. It is the Buckner's heart of a pastor that inspires this discussion. He is passionate about there being a translation that finds rather than loses would-be hearers and doers. This timely work will certainly give the reader something to ponder about faith that is authentic and user-friendly without throwing the baby out with the bath water. In times like these, we need a Savior that all can recognize and follow. Indeed, the timeless lyrics, "How to reach the masses, men [sic] of every birth! For an answer Jesus gave the key. If I be lifted up from the earth, I'll draw all men [sic] unto me," echo throughout the pages of this thoughtful and timely work. May the Lord add a blessing of clarity to the reading, hearing, and doing of this Word!

Rev. Dr. Ozzie E. Smith, Jr
Senior Pastor
Covenant United Church of Christ

PREFACE

In the movie, "Lost in Translation" Bill Murray is an American actor in Tokyo to film a commercial. While filming one scene the director - who could not speak English - was trying to give direction to Murray's character Bob, who could not understand Japanese. The director begins his comments by saying to the interpreter, "The translation is very important…" The director begins to say how Bob should feel and how he should look and the "passion" with which he should perform, even referencing another movie (Casablanca) to explain how he should look. The interpreter then looks at Bob and says "He wants you to turn, look in camera. O.K.?" Bob, knowing that he heard more than that, asks if that is all the director said to which the interpreter says yes. Thinking that is all the information, Bob asks if he should turn to the right or the left. The interpreter then asks the director, who begins again to explain the passion Bob should display, ultimately answering the question by saying, "Either way is fine. That kind of thing doesn't matter." The back and forth continues with Bob always getting the take wrong because of the poor interpretation of the interpreter. Often times I have found myself struggling to know the expectations of God for my life because I was acting based on the interpretation of the many interpreters that I grew up listening to. The more I read the bible, hoping to get a clearer understanding, it seemed like the less sense the words made. When I asked others about what God was trying to say to me I was resign to one seemingly insurmountable question. Did I understand the language of God, or am I just wrapped up in whatever the interpreter was giving to me?

In conversation with youth and "seasoned" believers in the congregations that I have been blessed to serve and worship with, I found some of my questions perplexed them as well. It was also not just likely, but probable that two people sitting in the same pew, hearing the same sermons, worshipping in the same ministry, are believing in two different Gods, such that their motivation for even being in the church is completely different. While one is moved by the fire and brimstone God, the other is moved by the loving grace of God. One goes home encouraged, the other leaves fearful that at any minute God will catch them "unready" and as a result are afraid to live. This simple example of two people in one congregation is a microcosm of what is happening in churches around the world.

Motivated by this thought, I began preaching and teaching on some of the unifying concepts of the bible. This exercise seemed to present change to those who heard it, but they often would ask about other concepts that I had not spoken about. Although I thought that most people would have more complicated questions regarding our faith, I was astonished to find that people who were "born and raised" in the church had difficulty grasping central biblical concepts.

Lost In Church Translation is my attempt to get back to the basics. This is not an attempt to define every biblical truth. Rather, this is a book that gives us basic biblical truths to grow from collectively. Each chapter is a mixture of sermonic notes and life observations that have developed my belief that at the heart of our expression is a basic love for God and as a result, a love for each other. While I could have taken a more academic approach to this topic, I think that it is more beneficial in this space to reach those of us who have no idea how to move from Paul of Tarsus to Paul Tillich. This is simply an opportunity for people to see the bible through its relation to real life, day-to-day examples. All of us have a socio-economic and cultural lens through which we read and interpret the bible and hear sermons. This is an attempt to broaden the lenses such that we can use a more universal perspective of the entire body of Christ, and not just the church we were established through. Theological terminology aside, people would like to understand how does a God which extends beyond time and space, a bible written many generations ago, and a Jesus who lived over 2000 years ago affect me and why should I care? This is not to disregard the debate and discussion amongst theologians to define each of the topics mentioned in this book. What it does is move us beyond the following of a traditional theologically-established belief and toward a place whereby we are unified by the words that precede two fundamentally challenging words; "God is…" Though some see this as a thought within itself, how we discuss or debate the words we put after this has shaped the division which has come to defined the most recent generation of church.

Not to give away the punch-line so to speak, but the basic purpose of this book is to clarify our faith in such a way that God ceases to be "either/or", but "both/and." Thomas Kuhn in his book, *The Structure of Scientific Revolutions* introduced the idea of what he called a paradigm shift. In order to explain his views regarding how we receive information, he used a picture that if looked at one way resembled an image of a duck and if seen another resembled a rabbit. He does not debate if the image is either a duck or a rabbit, but rather that the information we have informs which animal we see. What we tend to do in various religious communities is instead of accepting that truth, we debate whether or not the rabbit or the duck exist or is real based on our limitations. To explain it plainly, God is either a loving God who forgives us for our transgressions, or a God with a standard who chastises those who do not live up to those expectations. What this book proposes is that we see God as both and so much more!

I do not suggest you do away with your traditional practices and locally accepted beliefs. My prayer is that you find a place to conjoin your tradition with that of others, creating a path for your position in the church such that you don't "cut off your nose to spite your face." The human body has thousands of moving parts beyond the external (hands, feet, arms, legs, etc.). Each part has its role in allowing the body to function properly. Such is the nature of the body of Christ. My hope is that instead of being lost trying to understand each part of the body, you accept that we must work together to move in concert with the type of power given to us by God. Paul states to the church in Ephesus that, "[t]here is one body and one Spirit, just as you were called to the one hope of your calling, one Lord, one faith, one baptism, one God and Father of all, who is above all and through all and in all." (Ephesians 4:4-6) Following Paul's thought in Ephesians, *Lost In Church Translation* attempts to bring us back to this idea by giving us basic truths to find at the core of the more than 42,000 denominations and more than 450 version of the English Bible that will not leave a new convert or confused pew member lost in church translation. I challenge anyone that reads this book to not simply accept my perspective as truth, but rather use this as a launching pad to discover what it is that God requires and is speaking of you. Every prophetic word in the bible was not the same word. Every move of God in the bible was not a mirror image of another move. Every letter of Paul was not a repetitive word to each church, but there is truth to be found in each place. Take this book as an opportunity to find the unifying truth of God and not to reinforce our divisive opinions.

IT'S COMPLICATED

While sitting in the barber's chair, I have been a part of the most intriguing conversations. From politics, sports and cars, to clothes, shoes, you name it and it's probably been discussed at some point and time in the barber shop. Usually, I was the silent listener nodding as if I understood, but never engaging anyone in conversation. That is until church and God came up. Then I became actively involved. I was born and raised in the church which, I felt, made me an authority on the things it believes.

During one of my weekly shop visits, a guy screamed that he didn't believe in the bible, because it was written by men. I had heard this too many times before, so I raised an eyebrow as another man says that men wrote it, but it is God inspired. The first speaker said that didn't make sense. If a man had a pen, or feather, or whatever in his hand and wrote the words on the pages, he could easily lie and say that it was God inspired. I spent 10 minutes listening to their arguments hoping for a chance to say one thing and one thing alone.

After listening to this back and forth for a while, I decided to chime in with what I thought was the deepest thing that I have ever said in my life. I waited for a small break in the screams and said, "Y'all are being way too deep about this. If you believe in God, then believe in his word and if not, then don't." To which someone replied, "If it was that simple everyone would believe." We began down a somewhat deep theological debate discussing if it were easy to believe in God's word or if it were even possible to believe in something so great. With respect to God's word, the arguments ranged from the humanness of the writers, to the influence of religion and how it has allowed the book to remain relevant. Those discussions led us to the idea that we as humans don't have the ability to know all of God, and if we cannot know all of God then we cannot believe in God. My main argument was that one requires the other. You don't know someone unless you get to know them, and it is not in hearing them speak that you know them, but rather in understanding why they say what they say that helps you figure that person out. Understanding God was about accepting three things; 1) it requires faith; 2) faith requires that you believe in God; and 3) that in searching for God, you will receive the reward of God.

I eventually got them to concede to a certain degree with my ability to convert scripture into real life experiences, which was either greatly appreciated by them, or it annoyed them to the point that they just agreed to shut me up. Either way, the conversation was seemingly over. On my way out of the door, one of the gentlemen followed me out and began to ask more questions about faith and family. After a 30-minute conversation, he asked me a very interesting question. "What should we believe?"

To most that may seem like an easy question to answer. We will more than likely recite John 3:16 "For God so loved the world that he gave his only Son, so that everyone who believes in him may not perish but may have eternal life", or Romans 10:9 "because if you confess with your lips that Jesus is Lord and believe in your heart that God raised him from the dead, you will be saved." (I will speak more about these later.) For some strange reason I could not give him an answer. So my reply was simply to trust God and let that trust reveal what it is that God needs you to believe. As a preacher you know I had to give him a scripture with the word "believe" in it, but after he walked away I was left wondering to myself what should I believe? Not so much about God but rather what does it mean to be a believer.

As Christians, it is true that we are to believe in God's word as we are taught. However, there is an element of the faith that those who say this tend to forget. There is a divide that exists which makes it difficult for two people to believe the exact same thing. Amos 3:3, "Do two men walk together unless they have made an appointment [agreement]? (NASB)" Too often we stand in agreement with people without truly standing in full agreement with them. If I say to you meet me on Martin Luther King Drive at 4:00 p.m., there are several variables that we have to agree on. First, we must agree on which King Drive; every city in the United States has a King Drive. If I am in Chicago and you are in New York, and you go to King Drive and I go to King Drive we will both arrive at the correct street, but in two completely different places. Let's say for arguments sake we are in the same city. Then we would presume, all things considered, that cures everything, right? Well what about the proposition of 4:00 p.m.? What happens if it is the day after daylight savings time and one of us did not make the time change? Both of us may get there at four, but one will get there at their own perception of four. This is often the state of the faith. We stand in agreement on things without fully defining our agreeable terms, and as a result, we are feeding the world the same words, without feeding them the same message. Too often we expect people to understand what we say when there are often more variables to belief than a simple yes I do, or no I don't.

The proposition of a yes or no is typically developed through our maturation process. As we grow, we tend to gravitate to what it is we understand, and what we understand is shaped by what we are around. Put in a more palatable way, we are all, generally, products of our environment. I grew up around a family of gear heads - for those who don't know, that is a person who loves cars. As a result, as I got older I began to take an extreme interest in them. There is nothing that fascinates me more than the workings of a great automobile. Although there are many working parts in a car, there are some very basic things that you need to operate one. Also, no matter the style, manufacturer or brand of the car, they all hold some very basic parts. You need a well-maintained engine, a fully charged battery, and (as insignificant as they may seem, considering how often I lose mine) you need keys. The engine is the heart of your car. You can fix a lot of the other parts, but if the engine fully breaks down that is the point where you will need another engine, or car. The battery is the electrical charge for the car, and it is what gives power and life to the entire car. Finally, without a set of keys there is nothing you can do with the car, but look at it. Keys give a possessor access and authority to the thing they are used for.

As with a car, such is the relationship of a Christian with God. There are three basic things that you have to grasp before even venturing into any other part of your relationship, because as with a car, it would be impossible to move without these three things in line:

belief, love, and faith.

Belief

Belief is the basic foundation on which everything is founded. It is the engine of our relationships and what drives us to move in every area of our interaction with God. Everything that we receive, or do not receive from God is based first on what we believe is possible. In Mark 9, a man brings his son to Jesus' disciples to have him healed and delivered from a spirit that had afflicted him since his youth. The scripture says that the man asks Jesus if he can do anything, please heal his son. Jesus promptly replies, "anything is possible to him that believes." The man's reply is somewhat interesting in that he then says, "Lord I believe, help my unbelief." This man knew enough about Jesus and the works of his disciples to bring his son to him. He was persistent enough in that belief to stand in that position until he could get to Jesus, but evidently there was a great divide between his ability to believe in the works of Jesus and its application to his own life.

Often we believe that God can heal, deliver, save and fight, but we have a hard time believing that he can do all of those things for us. We believe in what Jesus did in the bible, but we fail to believe in his ability to do those things right now. As a result, we often become lost in the middle of everything we are taught and read to come-up with a big bag of information that is impossible to sift through. Then one day we gain enough understanding to know exactly what it is that we truly believe. The interesting thing about belief is that there are various things to believe and different ways to believe, according to the diverse set of beliefs used to establish new religions within the same grouping of people. Christianity is a religion with roughly 41,000 denominations to date according to the Center for the Study of Global Christianity at Gordon-Conwell Theological Seminary. That is 41,000 changes to a set of beliefs and standards. Trying to sort through it all makes it difficult to know what it means to say that I believe without ever searching to establish what it is that you believe. Like the man in Mark 9, we are often left saying to God that we do believe, but we also have some things that it is impossible for us to believe. The simple solution to the issue of belief is to believe God, but even God gets thrown into the jumble of concepts that are often misunderstood. So I ask the question, what do you believe.

To understand the concept of belief, think about your understanding of people. There are many people connected to me including my parents, my siblings, my extended family, my friends, my co-workers, etc. If you go to each group and ask each who I am, you will get a different answer based on how or they connect to me. Each group is justified in their belief as to who I am because that is how they know me. While my parents know me as their son, my co-workers will never know me that way but only as a fellow co-worker. Just as my parents will never know me as a co-worker, but only as their son (unless I work for my parents, which would be weird for me and will only serve to complicate the point). God is identified by many people as many things. That is the beautiful thing about God. Whatever you think of God; however you find a connection to God, that is who God will be to you until you receive another revelation in a different light and context. In Exodus 3:14, God is defined in a manner that is the essence, or at least should be, of what we are to know. It simply states "Ehyeh asher ehyeh," or as translated in English, "I am that I am."

Entire books have been dedicated to this concept, but what I want you all to grab a hold of is "God is." Everything that you could ask for, everything that you could need in this life or the next, God is. The foundation of this world is based on God's existence. Whether you use the name Jehovah Jireh (The Lord will provide [Genesis 22:13-14]), or Jehovah Rapha (The Lord that heals, [Exodus 15:26]), or Jehovah Shalom (The Lord our peace [Judges 6:24]), you must come to a place to believe that God is that and so much more. God doesn't stop being everything simply because we stop believing that he is, just as you do not stop being your parent's child when you marry and become a parent. Bishop Noel Jones, author and Pastor of the City of Refuge Church in Gardena, California, once said, "God is everywhere, but He is nowhere unless you meet Him somewhere." God will only come as far to you as you will allow your belief to travel, because there are no limits in God. Be brave enough to believe in the totality of whom he is. Look in your bible, see everything that he is and has done for everyone and in every situation and be bold enough to say that he was, is and will be and do all of those things in your life. God can never be anything to you that you are not open to Him being.

One last point about belief: An engine will only go as far as the owner allows it to. Without regular maintenance and tune-ups, an engine will inevitably breakdown and be rendered useless. Belief is the same way. It is rare that you will hear this from the pulpit, but the truth is that you have to regularly reassure yourself of exactly what it is that you believe. Believe is translated as *pisteuo* in Greek. What this means literally is to be persuaded, or to place confidence in, or to be assured. As with many of us, everything that we hold to be true can sometimes be questioned because of circumstances or something that we are taught. A belief check is making sure that our beliefs are consistent with the God we serve. Reassurance is something that God gives regularly, but it also must be something that we seek. By consistently assuring yourself of your belief, you ensure that your belief is being lived out and not held within.

Faith

Belief eventually matures into the second thing that you must have a grasp of: faith. Belief is an intellectual version of faith. It is something that we hold true for one reason or another. Faith is best defined by the bible itself in Hebrews 11:1 where it says, *"Now faith is the substance of things hoped for, the evidence of things not seen."* Faith is the thing, as a battery to a car, which gives power to every other aspect of our relationship with God. The bible says in verse 6 of Hebrews 11, *"…without faith it is impossible to please God, because anyone who comes to Him must believe that He exists and that he rewards those who earnestly seek Him."* This tells us that faith is the presence of a belief in an invisible God and searching for Him anyway. Faith is what allows a person to look, beyond a circumstance, situation or any given set of facts and see the truth behind the facts. Faith develops a belief where there is a lack of natural proof to cause you to believe. It is at the intersection of faith and belief that we are forced to understand the difference between fact and truth.

Some would have you believe that fact and truth are synonymous to one another. You don't have to be a bible scholar to understand that they are not. One of my favorite movies is "Law Abiding Citizen." I know it isn't the most deeply spiritual movie, but it is entertaining nevertheless. In it, Jaime Foxx plays a prosecutor trying to convict a character played by Gerard Butler for a string of murders of people connected to his family's death. During two heated scenes while discussing the pending trial, Gerard begs to be placed on the stand in the trial of his wife and daughter's killer. He says to Foxx, "Put me one the stand. I know that they did it." It's to this statement that Foxx replies, "It's not what you know, but what you can prove." Facts can be manipulated to paint whatever picture that you want. Facts give a limited view, no matter how many you may have. Foxx's statement tells us that without a number of facts, it is impossible to prove something to be the case.

On the other hand, truth simply is what it is. The origin of the word differs depending on who we speak to. One thing that is accepted no matter the definition is the acknowledgement of truth. Truth goes beyond understanding and comprehension in a matter and says simply what a thing is. Believing it or not doesn't change its nature. Faith is established by truth. The gospel of John begins with an explanation, of the existence of God and his word. In verse 14 it says, "the Word was made flesh and dwelt among us full of grace and truth." It is understood that this is a revelation of the birth and life of Jesus. This concept is expounded upon in John 14:6 where Jesus proclaims, "I am the way, the truth, and the life: no man cometh to the Father but by me." Truth is the word of God as it is the ultimate absolute. To understand anything within a spiritual context, we need to have the ability to accept that simple fact. There is a saying, "God said it, and I believe it that settles it." It is this kind of faith that is needed to accept the truth that is God's Word. Now God's Word is not a phrase to be used to explain away any and all irrational, fanatical acts of extremism. The Christian faith and many others have been lost in the muddle that is the explanation and understanding of God's word. This concept will be dealt with at length in every chapter, so just remember one thing before going any further. As it relates to faith, without it, there is no God. Faith is the meeting place between our limitation and God's limitless power.

Love

Belief and faith are two heavyweight topics in the faith community. Most conversations between believers and nonbelievers begin and end with a discussion, or debate (or argument depending on how extreme the parties are) about belief and faith. Unfortunately, this pulls us away from the ultimate place where God resides: Love. Love is THE MOST misused word in the church and in the world, often because it is the most difficult thing to define as it tends to have a highly individualized meaning.

There is no way I could sum up the true meanings (yes, there are more than one) of this word in a short introduction, but I can simply say that God is love. I know that seems like a complete cop-out to define love with a simple scripture, but think completely about what I am saying. Put it this way; think about what God is to you. Now think about the God your parents talk about, and then think about the God your pastor talks about, then think about the God your friends talk about. I could keep going, but you get the point that God is everything to everyone, yet something specific to specific people.

I will dive completely into this topic in a later chapter, but for your understanding of this think about "Shrek." Yes, that Shrek! In a conversation with donkey, who happens to be my favorite cartoon character EVER, remember what was said about Ogres and onions. No, not the part about them stinking, but rather that they have layers. Love is a very layered word, as is God. My job at this point is not to explain it, but rather to place it at the forefront of your mind as you read along remembering that in everything love must, not should, but MUST play a role. It is by love that we are saved (John 3:16) and are kept. God's grace, mercy, salvation, deliverance, healing and peace all are a part of the vast universe that is His love. And as great as it is, it is in our capacity to show, receive and give that love!

1 Corinthian 13:13 points out that there are three things that persist: faith, hope and love, with the greatest being love. Not to detract from the scripture, I do believe that faith, hope and love are what endures. However, in order to establish any of them, we must first establish what it is that we believe. All confessions of faith, of love and of hope pour out of our hearts from a place of belief. Because we have warped what it means to believe and what we should believe, we have failed as a church and ultimately as a body of believers.

When cleaning, we often sit with a pile of scattered items and one by one review them and sort them into three places: trash, current use or storage. I am not attempting to get you to do anything more than to sort. It is an attempt to get you to see God, not through the lens of your reality or religious beliefs, but rather an opportunity for you to see and stand on what it is that you believe and allow that belief to become a part of what and who you were called to be. I do not suggest that I am an authority on all things, nor do I believe that this book is the ultimate guide about how to have a relationship with God. A relationship with God is so personalized that only God can show you that. My simple prayer is that after reading this book you're moved to go beyond the pulpit and find God in your everyday life, outside the four walls of the church, and find the God who has been lost in our translation of the Word through religion. While I do believe that this book was inspired by God, ultimately, as many Pastors often states, I pray that this book points directly back to the author and finisher of my faith. It is a clarion call for us all to go back to our first love. Watch and pray as this book attempts to revive, reveal and establish what was lost over time through years of misunderstanding and misinterpretations. Trust God and believe that He will reveal what he must to you, and as Jesus so frequently said, "He That Has an Ear!!!

WE NEED TO TALK: CONVERSATIONAL PRAYER

One of the hardest things to hear from the woman that you are with is a phrase that to this day shakes me to my core when someone says it to me. It's a phrase that in and of itself is not bad, but has often played itself out to indicate that I am in trouble. The phrase is, "We need to talk!"

I know that this may come as a surprise to most people that know me because I can be extremely talkative, but I tend to hate having conversations where I might get in trouble. It's not so much that I know that I will be called out for what I may have or may not have done, but rather not knowing where that conversation may go. I know that sometimes it may be an opportunity for us simply to get to know each other. Other times it's an opportunity for us to connect, and as great and perfect of a man that I am, sometimes - and it pains me to admit this - I am less than perfect and it is an opportunity for her to tell me all about it. (Hopefully you all know that I am not perfect and am joking at this point). I have found that the woman in my life may use that phrase not for us to talk, but rather for me to listen. While it is very true that she expects me to listen all the time, there are times when she simply wants my attention so that I am clear on where she is and what she needs. Though I know that our conversations can find a way to enhance our relationship, it still is a very intimidating thing to me.

Unfortunately, I used this approach in not only having conversations with my significant other, but it has also played itself out in my prayer life. Furthermore, I have found that it plays itself out in the modern day church. While many church leaders, preachers and teachers have taught series, delivered sermons and hosted conferences about the power of prayer, it is my contention that we have all moved away from the principle definition, purpose and power of biblical prayer.

Prayer, like my conversations with the woman in my life, is a form of communicating with God. Also, like those conversations, prayer can serve several purposes in the life and growth of a believer's walk and relationship with God. The issue or the danger in the church's current understanding of prayer is that it has been reflective of our ineffectiveness to grow the church beyond the four walls. I once was sitting on a bus, and I watched as a couple sat silently with an aura of anger all over their faces. The guy looked like he did not want to listen and the woman looked as if she had a tremendous amount to say. Suddenly, as if on cue, the man turns in his frustration and looks at the woman and says, "Go ahead and say it." Then she replies: "Now you want to talk! You didn't want to talk when I wanted to speak, and now that you aren't getting what you want, you want to talk." I submit that this is the state of the church. We ride along with God, and when we are not getting what we feel we need, or as we feel we deserve, we go to prayer in frustration asking him to speak. It's irresponsible for a believer to sit and expect God to speak when we only are willing to listen on our time.

There are very specific reasons that God seeks to communicate with us through prayer, but too often we neglect figuring out the reason, the purpose or even how we ought to pray. In 1 Thessalonians 5:17, Paul instructs us that we should "pray without ceasing." I am not sure about you, but that seems like a daunting request. I love to talk, and praying to God is encouraging to do, but all day, every day? I mean, even the apostles were only asked to pray for an hour. Further understanding of the word shows that God could not have meant what most churches believe, which is that we are to talk to God without ceasing. Prayer has to be more than a one way conversation. Prayer is not a monologue, but rather a dialogue. Sometimes the part of prayer that God wants is our ability to listen without ceasing.

Listening is something that believers must understand is not reserved for leadership, but rather is a requirement of being a disciple. Jesus said in John 10:27, *"my sheep hear my voice, and I know them, and they follow me."* It is impossible to follow a shepherd that you don't listen to. Many times we do what we believe is prayer, asking God what his will is in a situation and never stop to hear an answer. This would be the equivalent of calling someone, asking them how they are, what they are doing and where they are and hanging up the phone before they can respond.

The Lord's Prayer (Matthew 6:9-13) is typically used as a template to prayer. It has been taught that the substance of the prayer shows us everything that must be included in an effective prayer. While I believe that the prayer holds a tremendous amount of significance to men and women of faith, clearly it is not the only prayer that Jesus intended to be prayed. The prayer of Gethsemane (Mark 14:32-42) is one of the most powerful prayers in the bible and does not follow the structure of the Lord's Prayer. While it does contain aspects, the prayer's power does not lie in its structure, but its passion. Researchers have done studies on what it takes to be an effective communicator. Here is a list of seven concepts that can change the way you pray and God's response to your prayers.

Know what prayer really is.

It is impossible to do something when you do not know what it is. Often we take for granted things like prayer in the church because it is presumed that a person should come equipped with the ability to pray. No one walks into a new life knowing how to effectively communicate. We often tell members that they should talk to God the way they talk to their friends. There are too many problems with that statement to go into. Maybe in the next book! What we should glean is that learning to pray is simply not that simple. Take a newly-born baby. It would be ridiculous to expect a newborn to be able to tell you what they need and want in an articulable manner. Likewise, it is not responsible for us to presume that all believers know how to pray and communicate with God. Some struggle to speak their truth because they have spent a life time avoiding that truth. So while our spirits have the ability to intercede for us, many of us are unwilling to honestly say that sometimes the hardest person to be honest with is ourselves. When this is the case, the idea of praying to a God who some have been taught, will condemn us for that truth, it just does not seem like a reasonable request. Teaching prayer is essential to understanding God and our truth in a manner that forces us to confront our issue in ways that are healthier.

And in doing so we also understand that Prayer is not just about our issues but about building an open line of communication with God. We often are told to pray when we have a request of God. Sometimes the most affectionate prayers are those that are spent simply "getting to know" God. Prayer requires a level of attentiveness to the God you are praying to that would often render prayerful responses of awe and wonder. Telling God you appreciate the many blessing that have been bestowed on you, and the strength that you have had to endure the hardship is just as important as our prayers of need.

Even the disciples, who were followers of Jesus thought the topic was serious enough to ask to be taught how to pray (Luke 11:1). Communication is defined as "the process of transferring signals/messages between a sender and a receiver through various methods (written words, nonverbal cues, spoken words)." It is also the tool we use to establish and modify relationships. This is also the case for prayer. It is through prayer that we establish our relationship with God. It is also what is used to change our walk as God sees fit.

Manifest constructive attitudes and beliefs.

How convincing are your prayers to God? Do you speak from what you hope to be true, or that you know to be true? God wants to know that you believe that he is able to do whatever you ask. The types of prayers that God responds to are prayers of faith; prayers that are spoken from the heart with a level of certainty as you pray. Why ask God to do a thing that you have no confidence in his ability to do? Again, Hebrews 11:6 tells us, *"Without faith it is impossible to please God, because anyone who comes to him must believe that he exists and that he rewards those who earnestly seek him."* Do you believe what you confess, or are you speaking out of routine, or structure? Trusting God to do the impossible ensures that He will make it possible. But in order for belief to exist it takes a level of honesty, patience, sincerity and respect (reverence) for what you believe.

Also, you must be certain that your belief is in God's ability and not your own. Jesus speaks of the prayers of hypocrites in Matthew 6:8 where he says that they pray to be seen. Their motive is to be seen as a person that has the ability and power to speak to God. The truth is that God knows the secrets of your heart and the reward given by people will never amount to the reward of God's response to a sincere prayer that you pray in faith.

Make eye contact.

Here is a question. When you pray, what of God are you looking to see? Would you be satisfied with seeing the hand of God move, or do you seek more? Are you satisfied with seeing the things of God but never seeing God? This was one of the most difficult questions that I had to ask myself as I began to learn how to pray. I ran into the prayer that changed my perspective on praying. In Exodus 33, Moses goes into the tabernacle and is hidden in a moment of communing with God, but it was verse 11 that startled me. The bible records "the Lord spoke unto Moses face-to-face, as a man speaks unto his friend." For many people, this may not seem relevant, but one thing I have learned is that I need face time with God. I need to be able to feel like the father loves me enough to speak to me face-to-face, like a friend, and part of that connection is eye contact. Before I go any further please note that the scripture says that God spoke to Moses as a friend. The right to speak with familiarity is reserved for God and God alone. In speaking to your parent, you should be able to speak to them freely. But have you ever tried talking to your mother or father or grandparent as if they were one of your friends. My grandmother would always tell me that I could say anything to her but "don't get too familiar." God deserves reverence at all times, and even in seeking to see His face we must be careful not to "get too familiar." Now I am not saying that God literally comes down and we have a staring contest of sorts, but rather the presence of God is sought in a way that you feel as though you have his complete attention. The same feeling you have when you are talking and someone looks you in the eye as you speak.

The inverse is true as well. Be sure to give God your full attention when you pray. Seeking face time with God makes no sense if you are checking to see if someone is looking for face time with you on your iPhone or iPad. I hate when it is apparent that a person's mind is elsewhere when I am talking to them; it makes me less apt to speak, regardless of how important the conversation is to me. I believe the same is true for God. God will not speak until He knows that He has your attention. James 5:16b (AMP) says that the earnest (heartfelt, continued) prayer of a righteous man makes tremendous power available [dynamic in its working]. Earnest is defined as serious in intention, purpose, or effort. Eye contact does just that.

One last thing to note with this concept: seeking the face of God is a way of ensuring that he responds. The often repeated scripture in 2 Chronicles 7:14 is used to show people the power of humility, prayer and repentance, but often we forget that one thing that is included in that is the ability to seek the face of God. Seeking the face of God is required to get a response from God.

Be aware of what your body is saying.

It is evident throughout scripture that there is not just one position to be in when you pray. There are prayers that are given while kneeling, standing, lying prostrate, etc., but my as grandmother used to tell me, even though there may not be a right answer, that does not mean there isn't a wrong one. When I was a kid and my mother reprimanded me on the rare occasion I would be in trouble, whenever she believed that I was not paying attention, she would stop talking and depending on the magnitude of my transgression either pop me in the back of the head, or commence a full scriptural analysis of Proverbs 13:24. Then after she was finished "loving" on me, my attention became fully hers. Often our posture says the exact same thing to God as my posture said to my mother. We "pray" to God in passing or come to God after we have already made a decision and expect to get Godly results God then has no choice but to let our decision lead to His discipline.

Sometimes our body language says so much more than the prayers we speak. Often, communication can be stopped before it starts by body language that tells people you don't want to talk. Next time you go to pray, be sure to check to see if your spiritual posture is such that God knows you are ready to receive. *And* by posture, I am not speaking of how you stand physically, but rather if you are in righteous standing with God. Does your position with God oppose what you are saying to him? Do you say God I love you, but you actions say God I don't trust you? Does your mouth say God not my will, while you are actively seeking options? Be sure that every part of you is in prayer and not just your mouth because it is only the prayer of the righteous that availeth much.

Have the courage to say what you think!

There is a book entitled "Sun Stand Still" by Steven Furtick that speaks to our ability to have the faith of Joshua when he asked God to make the sun stand still. It takes faith to believe that you have the ability to speak to God. As crazy as they may seem, it really is that simple. Do not think that you are alone in being hesitant in thinking that God is so large that he does not care about you. David says in Psalm 8:4, "what is man, that thou art mindful of him, and the son of man, that thou visit him?" David is a "biblical giant," and he trusted that God would be with him to slay Goliath. He believed in God such that the bible records that he is a man after God's own heart. Yet this great man of God asks the question, "Why do I matter?" Do not let this hurdle stop you from praying. As a child, I used to hate asking my mother for anything. It is not that I thought that she wouldn't do what I asked, but rather I thought that my menial request would not matter in the grand scheme of her life. One day she told me that she could not give me something I needed if I never told her that I needed it. Further, she went on to say that I am her son, and if no one else cares about what I need, she does. God approaches us the same way. God cared enough to make you, to number every hair on your head, to know you before you were in your mother's womb, to have a plan specifically for you. If God thought enough of us to do all of that, we should be confident in knowing that he shall supply all of our needs.

God is waiting on us to be strong enough to pray for the impossible. A friend of mine once asked while preaching, "What would happen if we believed God for real?" A part of us getting to a place to believe God "for real" is by knowing where we stand with God and knowing that there isn't anything too hard for God. You will never know your limits until you go beyond them. There are no limits in God and the power of God, so there should not be any limits to our faith in what God can do. Until you believe it enough to ask it in prayer, the impossible will always remain unreachable. Be confident in God and watch Him go beyond what you had the ability to think, dream or imagine.

Practice!

Prayer, like everything, takes practice and time to learn and develop. As with good communication, you must learn how to speak before you know what to speak. As I previously stated, prayer always seemed like an intimidating thing to me. Most of the people in the churches I went to and my family were great at praying. They would open and close with what seemed like the right scripture, they included all of the key words and even threw in a few thees, thys and thous. It was frustrating because my prayers always seemed like they were immature ramblings and not a prayer worth the attention of God. What believers must understand is that prayer, as with everything, takes faith and practice. I mentioned before where Paul tells the Thessalonian church to "pray without ceasing." Taken in context, Paul is telling them all of the things that they need to do to be successful in the faith. The idea of praying without ceasing is simply being in a place of consistent communication with God. As in any good relationship, you don't know all the right things to say when you first meet that person. You don't know what things make them angry, or upset, or happy, etc., but you learn by effective communication. You learn good communication through communicating; likewise, you learn to have a good and effective prayer life by praying.

Develop effective listening skills.

Listening may be the most difficult concept to grasp by members of the faith community, and the church at large. We love to hear ourselves talk! Maybe it's just me, but when talking to God, I used to think that I had to get everything out while I had his attention. Never stopping to realize that God has called me to pray and give me direction or an answer, not to hear my complaints. I tend to forget that he knows everything and not stopping to listen is the most destructive thing that I can do. I had a friend whose elderly grandmother did not speak much, but when she did it was with passion and wisdom. It amazed me how people would just come over to her house and sit with her hoping she would say something that would change their lives. Conversely, we come to church, or go to our prayer closets seeking a word that may change our lives, and yet we are never silent or still enough to hear God is saying. Many of us rely so heavily on our leadership to speak the word of God that we forget that God has prepared a word for us too.

1 Samuel 3 tells the story of a young Samuel, and how when he heard the voice of the Lord he thought it was Eli. Eli, after realizing

that God was trying to speak to Samuel gave him the advice that the modern church needs to begin to incorporate in our prayers. We need to get to a place where our prayer in the presence of God is simply, "Speak Lord, your servant is listening!" Often when the presence of God is evident, we respond as Samuel did. When he first heard God call him, Samuel's response was "Here I am! You called me!" While it is important to know where you are and that you are called, it is of more importance to know where you are going and why you were called. God seeks an ear that is willing to hear before giving you a mouth that is ready to speak. As in the days of Eli and Samuel, the word is rare today. Not because God is refusing to speak, but because God is struggling to find a church that is willing to listen.

Corporate Prayer

One place I always thought that I could hear God speak was in what is known as corporate prayer. One of the first concepts that I learned from studying the bible was the "power of agreement." I would often recite on my way to church for prayer a short prayer that stated, "Lord you said where there are two or three gathered in my name, that you would be in the midst (Matthew 18:20). So since you said it, I believe it. Now show up and speak." Then I would get there, and people would truthfully be engaged in nothing more than a shout fest. It would be about who could praise the loudest and which minister would speak in tongues first. People gathered, but the truth is they were not gathering in expectation of hearing from God and so God allowed us to hear ourselves and never spoke. Corporate prayer is an important part of the vision, growth and health of a body of believers, but what has become lost is the true utility and purpose of corporate prayer.

One of my favorite stories in the bible is found in 2 Chronicles 20. The bible tells us that Jehoshaphat got word from individuals close to him that the Moabites, the Ammonites and others were coming to do battle against him and the people of Judah. I must stop here to point out two things. First, it was not King Jehoshaphat that saw the enemy coming, but it was people around him. Too often in the church we presume that the only person who can see the attack of the enemy is the pastor or others in leadership. Often this proves to be true because the pastor is the main person seeking to protect the kingdom of God and its people. Every believer has a responsibility to protect the house of God understanding "[f]rom the days of John the Baptist until now the kingdom of heaven suffers violence and the violent take it by force." (Matt. 11:12). Protecting the house of God is something we all should be seeking corporately, not expecting simply the Leader to be the only one capable of "sounding the alarm." Second, the enemy was clear to those who saw them coming. Confirmation can only be made with people positioned to see what you see. Corporate prayer positions us as a unit with the ability to confirm what we hear and see.

The story continues and says that when Jehoshaphat got the message, "he feared, and set himself to seek the Lord, and proclaimed a fast throughout all of Judah." The next aspect of corporate prayer that is being lost is the concept of corporate fasting. Prayer and fasting are always used in conjunction with one another. When Michael Jordan, the former NBA great if you did not know, gave his speech for induction into the basketball hall of fame, he stated that he could not have done anything without his partner in crime, Scottie Pippen. IT was clear that for the Chicago Bulls to become world champions it took Michael and Scottie to lead the team to victory. In that same way, it takes prayer and fasting to lead our success as a church. Attending corporate prayer makes no sense if you don't take part in corporate fasting. Matthew 17:21 tells us that there are certain kinds of fights that you can't win without doing both.

At the point that the people were together and had fasted together and purposefully began to seek the Lord is when He spoke, but one thing to note: Jehoshaphat got the message of the impending war, called the corporate prayer and fasting and yet God did not speak through Jehoshaphat. God spoke through Jahaziel, a man of priestly blood but just a man in the crowd. The last and most common mistake of the church that this story shows us is that you cannot restrict how God speaks. God may use you to speak through. That is why every member of the house is important to the cause. Do not presume that God will only speak through the leaders of the house, but trust that God will speak, and believe that he is able to do so through whatever means he deems necessary.

The approach of the church to prayer has been a bit peculiar. We come together once a week for corporate prayer and never wait to hear what God has to say concerning why we were brought together. More can be gained from corporate prayer concerning the direction of the church than any meeting. In meetings, we discuss our ideas and thoughts about a matter. In corporate prayer we hear what God requires of the house. The church has lost the power of prayer because of our inability to collectively seek the heart of God and not just the presence of God. Corporate prayer, as it did for Jehoshaphat and Judah, should prepare us to take the necessary steps to do what God has called us to do. Sometimes we are not meeting to fight, but just to hear God say to us as he said to them, the battle is not ours, but His. Christians are so concerned with fighting that they forget one key to fighting is position. If we don't stop to hear what position God needs us in, we will fail. Maybe we should be holding up the arms of our leaders, maybe it is time to build, maybe it is time to stand, and maybe it is time to fight, but if you fight without the direction of God you will do so in vain. Seek to make corporate prayer a collective union of believers seeking the voice of God, not a shouting contest, and watch God reveal directions to your next level.

I'LL HAVE WHAT HE'S HAVING: GOD'S LIFE, GOD'S PURPOSE

Have you ever thought about how many things you use every day that you really don't know exactly how they work? You point the remote at your television and the channel or volume change or you adjust something to make the screen brighter, darker, but do you really know how it works or why it works the way it does? Like some of you I consider myself a man of innovation. I always seem to find a way to make something do what it was not meant to make it work for something I may need in that moment. For example, have you ever realized how many things you can do with a wire hanger? Really think about it. It can be a key to your car when the actual key is locked in the car. If your back itches you can use it as a back scratcher. I mean really think of the possibilities!

Unfortunately, some of us have treated our lives as I treat a hanger. We shift and shape it to do whatever it is that we need it to at the time without ever really taking the time to fully understand what it was meant to do and how it works. A wire hanger was made to hang clothes. The manufacturer never marketed the hanger as a back scratcher (although I am convinced that they should) because that is not what it was made for, even though it can be used that way. The manufacturer had something very specific in mind when it created the hanger. So too did your manufacturer when he made you. God created every last one of us with a very specific job in mind. He knew there were some things that needed to be done and so He created a tool that be used to fix the problem. When we take what God has given us and use it in ways it was not meant for, we become so comfortable with that use that we neglect its true power and purpose. Do you know how hard it is to hang clothes on a wire hanger that has been completely bent out of shape? Trust me, I have tried and failed. The sad part is that when I needed a wire hanger I could not find one, but I digress.

From blogs to books and signs to songs there is no shortage of information about the true meaning of purpose. So instead of debating or pulling together all that information, let's make this as simple as possible by pointing out and explaining several very integral and yet interesting things. First, your purpose is not about you. Second, gifts are God's tools in us to guide us towards our purpose and not necessarily into our purpose. Third, passion and purpose are more connected than your gift and purpose. Lastly, (and possibly most confusing so just take it and trust me when I say it will make sense later) your purpose is not yours to complete. Okay breathe. Now let me break this down.

First, the one thing that we all must understand is something that God explained himself, which is He is not a respecter of persons. Essentially what this means is that the sovereign reign of God is just that, sovereign. One of the greatest things God ever created just so happens to have occurred in my lifetime: The Cosby Show. For a kid like me, it became a ritual to sit and see what life would be like to have two funny, full of energy parents that just understood everything and nothing at the same time. I don't know anyone that did not try to live their lives vicariously through the Huxtables. One of the best episodes was when the parents Cliff and Claire (even their names were cute) were trying to show their son Theo the importance of trying his best after he gets bad grades in school and decides that he wants to be a "regular" person. At the end of the show, Theo makes an impassioned speech about how his parents should accept his decision. He ends by saying "So instead of acting disappointed because I'm not like you, maybe you can accept who I am and love me anyway, because I'm your son." At this point, I was overwhelmed with euphoria thinking I could be what I wanted and who I wanted, and my mother just had to deal with it. That feeling lasted all of two seconds as Cliff gave now the classic speech by saying, "That is the dumbest thing I have ever heard in my life!" He finishes by telling Theo that he is going to try his hardest because he said so, quipping the now infamous line that I heard a million times, "I brought you in this world, I can take you out!"

Understanding Cliff's stance should help you understand something about God. Regardless of what we feel God should accept, ultimately, it is God's job and his job alone to be God. As such he controls and decides what should and should not happen in and for our lives. What this essentially means is that the purpose for your life is for God's use, not your own. I know this is not a novel idea or concept, but place that thought into perspective. We continually look at God as the God of our lives and the God over everything. The Bible goes to painstaking lengths to remind us of something that we neglect to realize. God was more than the God of Abraham, he was more than just the God of Isaac, and even still more than the God of Jacob. Our God thinks, sees and breathes through eternity. While he is careful and loving enough to see us in our immediate need and sympathize with our infirmities, he also needs, sees and thinks on a level that is greater than our immediate issue and need. What God says in Isaiah 55 truly exemplifies this perspective: "As the heavens are from the earth, so are my thoughts higher than your thoughts."

If you have ever looked out the window of a plane you understand from that perspective you can see so much more than people on the ground. As such, you look to see everything that is happening under you. Conversely when you are on the ground, your concern goes no further than the space that you can see touch and feel. For some of us when we hear what happens in less fortunate areas it does not move us to action because we do not see it. On the other hand, people who have been to these places have great compassion because they have seen the issue and touched it. This means that because of God's perspective he cannot afford to make our purpose so individualized that it does not and cannot affect everything else that he sees. This includes your family, your community, your children, your grandchildren. God gave you a purpose that should change and affect people generations after you. The church often gives so much importance to the individuals that we miss the use of the whole, to the point that we equate the strength of a church with members, budget size and budgetary use. We give so much credit to how much a person does that we care more about them being active than we do how they are active. God uses us to reach others. A mechanic values his tools, but does not require every tool for every job. We are all tools in God's tool shed waiting on God to use us where we are needed.

The fact that we are tools to be used by God leads to my next point. God, in creating the tool, gave us various gifts. In this way as we are to God, our gifts are to us. Gifts are our tools to maneuver through the purpose of God for our life, but our gifts are not our purpose. When you think of this point, think of David. David has to be one of the most talented people in the entire bible. He could sing, write, play the harp, he was handsome, he was strong, he had everything, and yet his story starts as a shepherd. It is as a shepherd that he receives the calling of a King. Now if you understand David's culture and lineage then you know that going from leading sheep to leading a nation is an extreme leap that took a lot of maneuvering by God. Without recounting the story, God uses every gift that he gave David to promote him from a shepherd to a king.

In Proverbs 18:16 Solomon explains, *"A man's gift makes room for him and brings him before great men."* What the scripture is saying is that your gifts are used to create opportunities but are not the opportunities. Look at gifts as your keys to the levels within the purposes of God. There are certain spaces that you cannot access without your key. This concept will be explained later, but you must understand that the gifts that God gave us as individuals are for the purpose of gaining access to opportunities. Those opportunities are where God's true purpose lies.

Thomas Jefferson once said that most people do not take advantage of opportunities because they come dressed in overalls and look like work. The truth is it requires effort to live in purpose; effort is what separates the called and the chosen. God calls those that he has gifted and chooses those who work their gifts. There was a young man that I knew growing up who I believed was the best basketball player ever. I looked up to him as a kid. I believed if given a chance he could beat anybody in the NBA. On the other hand, there was a young kid that I knew as well who was a little bit younger than me. He was just plain horrible! He could barely dribble, couldn't shoot, was uncoordinated and a complete joke on the court. The first guy we will call Al and the younger we will call Bart. Because of his natural basketball acumen, Al could walk on the court and do whatever he wanted. As a result, he spent more time hanging out with the local drug dealers than he did working on his game. Meanwhile, I would go to the park or the gym late at night and Bart would be there with whoever he could pull out to watch him play ball. He worked and day-by-day he got better and better. Then all of a sudden, Bart began to have growth spurts. Next thing you know, little horrible Bart became a Division 1 basketball player. For those wondering what happened to Al, he did not get shot, he didn't go to jail. He settled in life, coasting through everything since he was gifted. This was when I learned that work is always greater than talent, and effort greater than any opportunity.

Opportunity is a funny thing. If you place opportunity in capable, willing and hardworking hands then the possibilities are limitless. A piece of canvass in the hands of an artist can become the Mona Lisa. A piece of paper in the hands of a thoughtful, impassioned person can become a speech about a dream. A piano and its keys become a tear jerking ballad. Opportunity is only valuable in the hands of a person that can see and fulfill the possibilities. Conversely, the same opportunity in hands that see obstacles and not possibilities is wasted. There is a story of a shoe salesman who wants to expand his company to other countries. He sends his best salesperson to a small village in Africa. The salesman spends a week there and then sends a message back to his job saying, "Send me a ticket to come home, these people don't where shoes." A few months later, as punishment for a poor job the boss sends another salesman to the same village. After an hour in the village, the man sends a message back home that says, "Send me all the shoes you have! These people do not have shoes!" Opportunity is only as great as the possessor. God places us in situations to use what he has gifted us to do, but without the fire and passion to do it, we are just wasting time. To this point, we must understand that it is our passion that drives us to the purpose of God.

Often we are taught in the church that we are to seek the peace of God to confirm the move of God. The truth, biblically, is that often it is in our discomfort, it is in our struggle that we find out exactly where God requires us to be. In Galatians 5:17, Paul states that *"the flesh sets its desire against the Spirit, and the Spirit against the flesh; for these are in opposition to one another so that you may not do the things that you please."* In this walk toward purpose, we must always remember that no matter how far along in our walk with Christ we are, we are a living contradiction. We have dueling realities that are ever present in our mortal bodies, and that is where we meet our frailty. God created us to be perfectly imperfect. He created us with flesh in a world that would lead us to desire things contrary to his will. He created us with feelings that we are told to tame. He created us with emotions that we must learn to ignore. My belief is that it is in these things that we find our true calling and God's purpose. Pastor Dr. Jamal Bryant of Empowerment Temple in Baltimore, Maryland once stated, "When you bump into your emotions, you will have a collision with your mission!" It is in the places that we find ourselves emotionally drawn that God is calling us to. The word passion is translated from a Greek word that means to suffer (*pashko*). It is in the place of our suffering that we are drawn to change what causes the suffering. It is in our suffering that we encounter the will of God and it is in the will of God that we see the eternal place of God's purpose.

John 3:16 tends to be a very familiar verse to note as it relates the love of God, but look deeper into the scripture. The sacrifice of Christ was bigger than you and me. I know that is what we love speaking, decreeing and declaring in the church, but what if God's plan was bigger than you and me; bigger than our failings, greater than the flesh and more specifically the sin that we allowed into his plan. We will deal with this at a greater level in a later chapter, but what God "hates" is what God defeated. What God did not want in his plan, he removed from his plan. That plan included everlasting life, abundance, peace, joy, all of the things that he created in the garden for us is what sits on the other side of God defeating what angers Him. As with God so too is it with us. Every time I complain about something A friend of mine always replies, "You have to be the change that you want to see." The very things that we are called to change God placed in us to hate, and hate to the point that we would desire to change it. What we tend to do is run from what we hate, yet it is the recovering addict that can reach the addict. God saw what was needed and decided to be the change He wanted to see!

Now if, you read this chapter carefully you will notice that I never use the phrase, your purpose. Purpose speaks to a complete view; a view that can only be had from the perspective of one who has a view of the end of a thing. We were chosen by God to run in a direct path. While God will give us visions for what we shall do in this life, I challenge each believer to understand that vision is not purpose. Vision speaks to perspective, while purpose speaks to an end. It is for this reason that it is not possible for the purpose of God to be completed by us. We are God's vessels and we are his tools, yet it is the hand of God that brings us to a place where the purpose he has planned is completed. We must be satisfied knowing that God will use all the tools when he requires them, because we can never know exactly what God requires of the tool. If we understand this point, then we will find comfort in knowing that our purpose is God's will, and, as such it is for God to complete.

Now this is not an excuse to be lazy, but rather to play your position. The mechanic fixes a car, but uses his tools to do the work. The mechanic places his hand on the tool and guides the tool to do the work. The point is that God has a greater purpose than we have the opportunity or ability to see. It is our job to tend to the work of this generation, so that those who follow after us will not be starting from behind. There is work to do that will allow the next stage of God's plan to be completed, but we are to simply prepare. The person who cuts the tree down rarely sees it turned into lumber. The one who makes the lumber does not design and build the house. The one who builds the house rarely if ever lives in the house. And the first owner rarely if ever sees the improvements made by the second, third or fourth owner. Each person in that chain had a job and each person after it needed that job to be done in order for them to do theirs.

There is a great work to do, but it is God who leads us to our assignment, to the fulfillment of his purpose. Abraham was to be the father of many nations, yet the nations were "fathered" through his grandson Jacob, now known as Israel. Moses was to deliver Israel to the Promised Land; he delivered them from Egypt, but never saw the Promised Land as Israel was brought to the Promised Land by Joshua. David purposed in his heart to build a temple, but the temple was built by his son Solomon. All of them wanted to see the kingdom of God on earth, yet the Kingdom came with Jesus. We all will see God's purpose fulfilled, whether it be by his side or not, but always remember to be *"confident of this very thing, that He who began a good work in you shall complete it until the day of Christ Jesus!"* (Philippians 1:6)

SEEING THINGS: VISION

There is a story of a bird that chose not to fly south for the winter. The bird swooped down to where he saw food and after he ate he realized that he was now stuck. Suddenly, a cow came and saw the bird. The bird screamed out to the cow asking for help getting unstuck. The cow then, defecated on the bird, so now the bird was covered in feces. That is when a cat came and saw the bird in the feces and decided to pick the bird up and clean it off. Once it was cleaned off, the cat killed and ate the bird. What does this mean? Everyone that puts you in a mess is not hurting you and everyone that gets you out of mess is not helping you.

The greatest hindrance and asset that you can have in your journey is the people who have access to you. If you allow short sighted people to have access to you, then you run the risk of seeing life through their eyes. Visionaries surround themselves with vision-filled people. Do an evaluation of your access points. When Nehemiah went to rebuild he did not rebuild Jerusalem, he rebuilt the wall around Jerusalem. In biblical times, a city built a wall around it for two primary purposes: to restrict what could come in, and to control what came out. It was a city's defense mechanism and a way to govern the things that were in it. Many of us are living a life without walls or without restriction. We must gain a modicum of self-control for the bible says in Proverbs 25:28, "*A person without self-control is like a city whose walls have been burned down.*" Vision is what allows us that level of control because it becomes about a greater picture beyond what we can see.

After a very interesting discussion with someone, I was forced to take a long look at a lot of things. The one thing that God spoke most loudly about was the difference between seeing the truth and knowing the truth. Situations and Circumstances always lend itself to a person drawing conclusions. We have often heard the phrase, "If it walks like a duck, quacks like a duck and looks like a duck, it's a duck." However, as we grow older we learn that life and truth are a lot more complicated than that. What you see may not necessarily be what you get, or as a friend of mine reminded me, we are to believe half of what we see and none of what we hear. Which brings me to my point: there is a great difference between sight and vision.

The primary duty of a person with faith is to look beyond what they see and hold fast to what they believe. Because of a lack of faith many of us fail by allowing our circumstances and things we see to dictate the decisions we make. We put our response under an answered prayer, or by saying "everything happens for a reason." The truth is everything does happen for a reason, but rarely is it for the reason we believe, and it's at this crossroad that we are introduced to vision. Sight gives you access to the circumstance; vision gives you access to the purpose behind the circumstance. Vision (or *chazown* in Greek) means a divine sight given by God. It is the ability to glance at what is happening from God's perspective. Now before going any further, please note that you must have access to God before having access to the vision of God, but I digress. Sight is natural, vision is spiritual and it is also a gift. We can't continue to look at what we see and believe simply because the circumstances dictate such. That concept works both ways. Just because something appears to be right does not make it right, and simply because something looks bad does not make it bad.

I will not belabor the point, but what I learned, simply from one conversation, is that people will always see what they want. Regardless of change, sight restricts the ability to have a vision. To have one, you must forsake the other. Success as a Christian and in life is dictated by what we do or say, and typically what we do or say is determined by what we see. Next time an opportunity arises for you to choose, my prayer is that you will use God's vision, and not your own ability to see. Here are some tips to help with this change. First, remove all other persons from the decision process. The only voice that matters is God's, so allowing others to chime in on your process makes absolutely no sense, as they do not have the vision for your life. God can speak through people, but confirms what he says away from the speaker. This is my biggest issue with people's use of social media. We post pictures; we express ourselves openly in hopes that people will comment or read our information and like what we say or how we look. No one has ever intentionally put up a comment or picture that they hope no one would comment about. So if that is the case, what is it that we are doing with this information? How do we allow what others have going on to affect how we feel about our own lives? It is my belief that contacting is not the same as connecting, and unfortunately social media blurs the line between the two.

People have thousands of friends that comment, re-tweet, poke and like what we place on these sites, and often we defer to the group as to whether something is good or bad. Sometimes people go as far as asking personal questions and advice of people with no real knowledge or understanding of who they are, or who our God is. We get all this information and depending on the sources we act on the advice. What we wear, think, aspire to have is somehow connected to what others think, want and desire. Using social media to get out a message is one thing, but using it as a barometer for your life which is what most people do is counterproductive to living with God's vision. Now I know what some of you may think, "Well this does not apply to me because I only have friends, followers and follow people that I know." Well here is a test. Go down your list of friends, followers, etc. and count the number of people you can trust. Not just a simple trust, but I can trust with my inner thoughts, feelings and emotions. I guarantee that you will struggle to find half of your few hundred or few thousand friends fit into this category. We can't share ourselves with these people and yet we share our intimate moments with them. We also allow them to comment and rate those moments at their leisure and at times, at the expense of our pain. Social media causes us to have our conversations of life with the world before we have it with the God who has prepared a plan and vision for the life we post, Instagram and tweet about.

This brings me to my second and main point. Pray early and often! Do not wait until you are fully engulfed by a situation or circumstance to ask God what should be done. Before you marry that person, before you become friends, and for you social media people, before you accept that friend request, make that comment or post that picture, check with God because sometimes the smallest thing can turn into your quickest destruction.

Lastly, wait for an answer FROM GOD! Most times we think that what a person does is God's way of answering a question when that can't be further from the truth. God speaks for God! Think about it in the context of relationships. Because he bought the right flowers and treats you well does not mean that he is the one. Just because she lied doesn't mean that she isn't. God typically uses the most flawed people to do His will in the earth, and yet it is the flawed people that we tend to reject. If God rejected the people that we tend to reject today, then we all would be outcast from God's presence, including me! An alcoholic built the ark. A murderer and stutterer delivered Israel. An adulterer and conspirator to murder was the King of Israel and a man after God's own heart. An polygamist and easily influenced king, was the wisest man the world has ever known. We cannot allow a person's fault to disqualify them from being used. The love of God can change a person, but it is easier to turn away what we don't agree with, than understand the issue. Remember Psalm 118:22, *"It was the stone that the builders rejected that became the chief cornerstone."* Listen for the will of God and that will ensure that you are working from vision and not sight.

WHAT'LL YA HAVE: SERVING

Anyone that enjoys a good restaurant knows there are three extremely important things that determine whether or not you return. The first is how clean it is. I am not sure if I can have a great dining experience in a place where the table and floors are dirty, and when I get my plate I have pieces of roast beef stuck on the plate when I ordered a Chicken Caesar Salad. I mean, at least you can clean the plates, right? Sorry, that is an emotional topic for me. Second is the food. Nasty food is just that, nasty.

More than anything that can make or break a dining experience is the service. I never fully understood that concept until I stepped foot in a restaurant that shall remain nameless that completely shaped my thought process about this. Between the long wait to order, the cold food that was brought to my table and several other issues, I could barely sit there for long before expressing my frustration with the service to the manager. When the manager arrived, I explained to him all that was wrong with the service and how the server was treating me. After my monologue, the manager kindly replied that the restaurant does that intentionally for an enjoyable, comedic meal. After hearing him say that, I realized that all of the servers were like that. Some tables even had the patrons interacting with the servers in an equally rude way.

Unfortunately this funny scene has found its way into the church, without the acceptance of our manager, God. Service has taken a backseat to our roles within the church. We have come to accept any and everything as acceptable service. This is cause by a misunderstanding of what it means to be a servant versus being a server.

A server serves without attachment. They seek to fulfill a request. A server delivers an outcome, but does not necessarily do the work required to produce the outcome. Conversely, a servant is bound to the person they serve. A servant doesn't simply wait on the request, but rather they look to meet the need before the request is made. A server has no real obligation to the person they serve. A servant's life is dedicated to whom they serve. Very simply put, God called us to be servants, not servers.

What exactly separates a servant from a server? As a kid you are told that you should do what your parents tell you. I learned that the truth is as a kid we are taught to do what is told, when it isn't actually said. I am not sure about you, but it took my parents to ask me to do something before I did it. If they wanted my room to be cleaned, they would ask and I would clean. If they wanted the garbage taken out, even if it was overflowing, if they wanted me to do it, they would ask, and I would take it out. Unfortunately, these me to many tension-filled encounters with my parents. I am sure many parents are possibly reading this and saying, well if you saw that it needed to be done why did someone have to tell you to do it? Well parents that is my question to you and everyone. In a world where the need is apparent, why is it that we have to wait on God to tell us to do something before we do it? There lies the difference between a servant and a server. A server only does what is requested. They never go beyond the bounds of a request to ensure that the needs of the person that they are serving are met. A servant requires a connected relationship between the servant and the master by which the expectations of the needs of the master is met before the need becomes necessarily evident.

A great example of the difference between the two is found in Luke 10:38-42. The story reads:

"Now as they were traveling along, He entered a village; and a woman named Martha welcomed Him into her home. She had a sister called Mary, who was seated at the Lord's feet, listening to His word. But Martha was distracted with all her preparations; and she came up to Him and said, "Lord, do You not care that my sister has left me to do all the serving alone? Then tell her to help me." But the Lord answered and said to her, "Martha, Martha, you are worried

and bothered about so many things; but only one thing is necessary, for Mary has chosen the good part, which shall not be taken away from her."

Now at first glance it appears that Martha is the servant as she is moving and Mary is the server as she is simply listening. But in understanding the circumstances you must see two things. First, Jesus is on his way to the place where he will be crucified. Jesus is preparing for what he knows to be next. To that end, Mary is sitting at the feet of God seeking to hear everything that he has to say, at the chance that she will not see him again. Martha is running around the house trying to prepare the house and serve her guest while Jesus is in her presence. Then in disgust Martha asks Jesus, if he cared that she was doing all of the work. And before He could answer she requested that she tell Mary to help her. Jesus' reply is very telling in that he told Martha that she is concerned with a lot of things while Mary is doing what is "necessary." Nowhere in the scripture do you see Mary ask Jesus what is necessary, but her connection to him put her in a place where she knew. So many times we as Christians become so weighed down with the thought of everything that appears to need to be done; we reason why certain things should receive our attention and neglect others as they are not an apparent need. The place of a servant is reserved for those that are in relationship. That relationship is a required step to being a Christian. Paul sheds light on this thought Philippians 2:1-8 gives a very descriptive look at how Christ lived as our example:

"If there be therefore any consolation in Christ, if any comfort of love, if any fellowship of the Spirit, if any bowels and mercies, Fulfill ye my joy, that ye be likeminded, having the same love, being of one accord, of one mind. Let nothing be done through strife or vainglory, but in lowliness of mind let each esteems other better than themselves. Look not every man on his own things, but every man also on the things of others. Let this mind be in you, which was also in Christ Jesus: Who, being in the form of God, thought it not robbery to be equal with God: But made himself of no reputation, and took upon him the form of a servant, and was made in the likeness of men: And being found in fashion as a man, he humbled himself, and became obedient unto death, even the death of the cross."

I once had a friend who had a girl break up with him for what seemed like the dumbest thing I have ever heard in my entire life. I literally thought she was just creating a reason to end their relationship. She broke up with him because whenever he would brake hard in the car, he never placed an arm over her to hold her back in the seat. Some of you may be thinking the exact same thing I was thinking: that is just plain stupid! Because, I knew the woman as well I called her. She told me not placing an arm over her meant he cared more about his safety than he did hers. She did not want to date a man she could not see herself marrying and could not marry a man who did not have her best interest at heart. Unfortunately, we all suffer from a self-serving perspective. We have grown more self-serving in a faith that asks us to serve each other. We seek ways to grow our ministries, instead of forwarding the faith of the collective body of Christ. This is one of the main reasons why we have more people in the church today, but less power. People have grown accepting of the "self-help" approach to our relationship with God and the church. We seek the presence of God and we serve in order to get "my blessing," "my faith," and "my salvation" at the cost of the interest of the whole. Our concern with serving the house of God and the people in it has become about serving our house and the people in it.

The true issue is that we have few servants with power, and that is the point of this chapter. It is less about the divide between the harvest and God's laborers, but rather teaching the few how to serve with power. There are three things that a person must do to serve with power: choose to serve, seek to serve and serve to destiny.

Choose To Serve

The first thing you must do is choose to serve. That sounds so generic, but the choice is more than just choosing to do something. I know what we hear from the pulpit is "just do something," but you must understand that your choice has somewhat been made for you. Further, you must understand that where you were called to serve, you have been gifted to serve there.

Take a look at these two scriptures. First Joshua 24:15:

"But if serving the LORD *seems undesirable to you, then choose for yourselves this day whom you will serve, whether the gods your ancestors served beyond the Euphrates, or the gods of the Amorites, in whose land you are living. But as for me and my household, we will serve the* LORD.*"* Now look at Matthew 6:24: *No one can serve two masters. Either you will hate the one and love the other, or you will be devoted to the one and despise the other. You cannot serve both God and money."*

If you look at this scripture intently and the context of these comments by Joshua and Jesus, you will understand that choosing to serve speaks to the intent of a thing and your faith in that intent. God places the intent of our service in us, and aligns our experiences to prepare us for that service.

Have you thought about the reasons the bible says that God gives his gifts without repentance? As a kid, I always wanted to understand why not allowing a child to use something was punishment. I mean as a kid we are taught that if something is ours it's ours and even if our parents take it away after the punishment period we can use it again. Misusing a gift does not remove the gift because as stated, it is your gift that makes room for you. God equipped us fully to do what we are called to do, and if he removes the gift the reconciliation could not be complete because we could not function as God has called us to.

The problem is we have people looking to have a job that God did not gift them for or call them to. God will only hire those equipped to do the task. Now to be equipped does not mean that I have to be great or even good at it, but rather I have the capacity to do what God has called me to do. Let me make it even simpler. If you go to a theme or amusement park, certain rides you have to be a specific height to ride. There may be a lot of other rides you can get on, but there is still a handful of rides that you cannot ride. If you have to be 6 feet and God stopped your growing at 5 feet 10 inches then you will never ride the ride meant for a 6-foot person. That does not mean you cannot get on every other ride in the park, but that ride was meant for someone your height. Every "job" in the body of Christ is not meant for everyone. Choosing to serve first must come with an understanding and knowledge with of how God has called you to serve.

Last point with this is often we don't choose to serve because we don't get what we feel we deserve out of it. We expect the pastor or first lady to notice it and reward us. Your reward for serving is the peace that comes with being confident in what you are doing. When you choose to serve, you have to keep in perspective you are choosing to serve. This is more of an issue of understanding, because we become frustrated in our service and in other areas of our lives because we are serving things and people that don't have the capacity to appreciate it. So you feel unappreciated at a job and spend your day on job search websites because you work in a place where you feel like you are serving in vain. Even the bible discusses this in Matthew 7:6 where it says, *"do not give dogs what is sacred, do not throw your pearls before the swine, if you do they may trample them under feet and then turn and tear you to pieces."* The key point to keep in mind with this is that your reward will come from who you choose to serve. If you serve people, then you will receive a reward from people. When you serve instead remember Colossians 3:23-24: *"Whatever you do, work at it with all your heart, as working for the Lord, not for human masters, since you know that you will receive an inheritance from the Lord as a reward. It is the Lord Christ you are serving."*

Now in choosing to serve we must be careful that we do not allow control issues to be a factor in our choices. I believe the idea of not having control creates a fear in Christians today that paralyzes them. Fear of the unknown not only keeps Christians from allowing God to be Lord, but it also stops many Christians from walking in the fullness of the power given to them by God through prayer.

We seek the voice of someone we can't see to learn how to deal with an issue or problem that we do see. If we really think about it, it is when we take control of our life that things become more complicated and confusing. Jesus explained this in great detail in Matthew 6:25-34. We find ourselves worrying about things and God never intended for us to worry, but this is the life that we choose for ourselves when we have control.

The problem of struggling with control isn't what we see, but rather what we choose to give our attention to; this is why it is of the utmost importance for us to be aware of the weight of what we are seeing. May I suggest there are many people who can see a situation but not be aware of the full meaning of it. You may see that you don't have enough to pay your bills, and, as a result, you consider the worldly options to find a way to meet your needs. As Christians, if in that same situation, we SHOULD BE aware that not only is God our Savior and not only is He our Lord, but He is also our Provider. This is not a suggestion to ignore your circumstance, but rather consult God who can guide you into the correct way to address the issue or concern.

Seek To Serve

The year was 1996. I was in eighth grade. My school had made the playoffs for basketball and we had to play St. Dorothy. The game was highly anticipated as we were the two best teams in the Catholic League Conference. The game was tight the entire time. There were nineteen seconds left in the game. I go up for a jump shot and I am fouled. I missed the shot, but we were only down one with me going to the line for two. Up to that point I had a pretty good game and I was a pretty good shooter. I shoot and make the first. Then I make the second. We are up by one. St. Dorothy does not call a time out. They take the ball the length of the court and lay it up. There is now eight seconds left in the game. We call a time out. In the huddle our coach asks one simple question, "Who wants the ball?" Because I had a pretty good shooting game that day, all of my teammates volunteer me. Coach looks at me and says, "Ok go get the ball and take a good shot." Looking back that was not a great plan, but I digress. We take the ball out. I stand on the complete opposite side of the court and as the ref counts down my teammate is forced to throw the ball in to another teammate who is standing at half court. He forces a shot up, misses and we lose. After the game the coach walks up to me and says something I carry with me to this day: "Wanting to do something does not show that you are willing to do it. Your ability ends when you choose to not act."

Most of the church was just like me in that game. We have the ability to do a thing, but we never go beyond the bounds of our comfort zone to accomplish what we have chosen to do. We come Sunday after Sunday, sit in the same seat and at the end we leave and do little if anything to further serve God by spreading the word of God. It reminds me of my high school experience. I was a pretty bright kid and I wanted to graduate, but because school was easy I kind of coasted. I got pretty decent grades and was a part of everything that I could fit into my schedule, but often when I came to school I wasn't learning at all, I was just showing up. I never made the choice to do anything beyond what was easy.

Choosing speaks to your willing submission to serve, but at the point that you have made the choice, the question becomes what now? The choice means nothing without corresponding action. At church we walk into a room full of people who seem to know each other and listen to banter about what we should and shouldn't do then leave and go home without anything being done.

I will not force the point, but after choosing to serve the next decision you have to make is to find a way to serve. Go to your church leadership and let them know what God has called you to do and ask them where that can fit into their vision for the church at large. Now clear warning, do not say "God said…" if you don't know what God said. Leadership, for the most part, has a unique calling on their lives and most are very good at discerning the voice of God. If you are unsure about something, seek wise counsel and trust the direction that God gives you through your leadership.

Serve To Destiny

So you have made the choice to serve, and you are serving. Months, weeks, even years go by, and you serve. Now what? The answer to that question is simple: serve some more! Most of us get caught in what we call dead end service. Not because it is necessarily dead end service, but one of two things can be taking place. The first could be you are not serving where God called you to serve. Second could be that you are not positioning yourself as a willing servant as described through Christ in the aforementioned scripture in Philippians 2:1-8.

For clarity sake, let's say you are serving where God called you and how God called you to serve. If this is the case, then what is next in elevation to destiny? Now before I move forward with this idea, please understand that elevation does not mean a change in title or duty. What it means is that you serve, give over control and let God handle the rest.

Two people come to mind to further explain my point. The first is David. Take a look at David's story; he went from shepherd, to psalmist/harpist, to soldier, to captain, to exile, to king. At the beginning of David's story, he is anointed the next King of Israel. One thing that did not change after the anointing was the posture of David's heart. While he was a shepherd, he was the best shepherd. While he was a harpist he was the best. While he was a soldier and captain, he was the best and eventually the manifestation of his calling came into being. The key to this point is that his level of service was not dictated by his calling, but rather he allowed his service to move him into his calling and anointing. David is an interesting case because as he served, he was elevated; yet as he was elevated, his title changed. Does that mean that when we serve our title should change as well?

That brings me to my second person, the model of a servant that

I began this discussion with: Jesus. Now I know what some of you are thinking "Jesus was God so his title could not have changed." Well you are right, but I suggest the same can be said about you. The bible tells us that God knows our ends from our beginnings. It tells us that he knew us before we were formed in our mother's womb. So if this is the case, could it also not be the case that God knew the position you would serve in before you began to serve? Jesus' title as God and savior and the Christ was established well before Mary got a message from God. So to that end, how you serve and where you serve is used to move you closer to what God has already called you to. That should place you in a position to release control of your process and your life and trust God with your service with a smile.

THE POWER OF PRAISE

One of the topics that simply is not discussed enough in the church, but typically one of the first things that people are introduced to is praise. It seems like a simple concept, and to an extent it is, but there are many misconceptions that the church has with respect to its understanding of the concept of praise. When we think of praise, typically we relegate it to a few words and phrases and believe that it is praise. The truth is praise is a question of the condition of the heart. More people in the church are seeking opportunities to be praised instead of finding an opportunity to give praise. What makes praise difficult is the rigidity of it in the typical service. Praise has become nothing more than a game of Simon Says. The preacher or other leader tells you to lift your hands, shout or scream, and we simply do it. This, in the sight of God, is simply empty noise. Praise is one of the most powerful weapons a believer has, and yet it is one of the many tools that we take for granted.

Before diving into the truth behind praise, you must understand what it is. Praise as used in the bible can carry several different meanings. The overarching definition is to boast, shine or cast gratitude. Very simply, praise is an act of giving thanks for God and the things that he has done, is doing and will do. Many find it easy to give thanks for something that God has done as it pertains to our lives. It's not hard to give thanks to God for healing your body, or helping you through a rough period or something like that. The difficulty comes when you are asked to give praise to God for something that he is doing, or will do. The reason this can be a difficult thing is because typically you cannot see the hand of God moving on your life until he has already moved. Our vision of what God is doing is like that of a semi-truck driver. When I first learned to drive, I never understood what people meant when they said to me I needed to periodically check my blind spots. I never understood the concept until while in the car with a friend driving, a truck sideswiped his car. When talking to the truck driver about insurance information, he said that we were in his blind spot and he could not see us coming up on his side. When God does things in our lives, often he comes up on us in ways that we cannot see and because we can't see it, we choose not to believe (more about this later).

What we must understand is there is no prerequisite to giving a genuine praise other than being genuine. The 150th and last Psalm of David tells us how to praise, but it closes by telling us that everything that has breath can give God praise. Furthermore, he makes it clear that praise is something all people are required to do. Praise is how we magnify God. It is how we make Him great in our lives and in making Him great, we diminish the significance of the issues of life. Praise is not an emotional explosion, but rather a shout of confirmation. You don't shout from emotion, you shout to confirm to God that you know that it is from Him that every good and perfect gift comes. You shout and leap for joy because the victory over your circumstances has already been won.

Praise has far more usefulness than simply a sign of gratitude for God. Often God has used praise to activate the faith of people, as it is what does the miraculous. Whether it is a shout, a dance or a word, there are many things beyond what we usually see or hear that praise is and can do.

A Weapon of War
(Psalm 149:6-7)

I love watching old war movies. It is interesting to see how the soldiers would approach going into battle. One thing most armies did right before the fight broke out was to yell the most inaudible words phrases to scare the enemy. I found out these sounds are called battle cries. Sometimes battle cries served as a way of striking fear in the opposing armies. This is one way that praise works in war. A strong, confident praise can be used to place fear in the enemy and cause them to be hesitant in battle. The enemy always seeks to attack a praiser, not because a praiser is weak, but rather because a praiser has power and confidence in battle. Next time you praise God, let it serve as intimidation to the enemy. Make the enemy fear your praise.

Request the Presence of God
(Psalm 22:3)

Everyone loves to feel truly appreciated. It is easy to rest and abide in a place where you are needed or wanted. It is through our praise that we can show God both. Praise is the simplest way to request an audience with God. I once heard a preacher say that "God can never deny a worshipper." Praise says to God that you want nothing more than to show gratitude for what He is doing, has done and will do. The bible says that God inhabits (dwells) in the praises of His people. This statement makes it a truth that where the praises of God are, so is He. We often hear it stated that when the praise of God goes up, His blessings come down. The blessing that accompanies the praises of God is God himself. Not more material blessings, but the greatest blessing that you could ever receive: an audience with the God.

Brings Deliverance and Victory
(2 Chronicles 20: 21-22)

I am a huge basketball fan. While I do not have a favorite team, I grew up playing the sport and loved every part of it. It was always exhilarating when my team won, because that gave us a chance to release the tension of a hard-fought battle. We never wanted to celebrate the win before it happened because we thought that would make us lose focus. Being a Christian, often that mindset has been transferred into the world of deliverance and victory in a battle. Unfortunately, it is often our praise for the victory that we can't see yet that is what actually determines the outcome of the battle. Throughout the bible, there are instances where God allowed people to praise while he fought. The account in the aforementioned scripture in Chronicles tells of how Jehoshaphat and the people of Judah and Israel praised God on one side, while the enemies that came to fight them were destroying themselves on the other side. Although it sounds like a cliché because of its use in the church, it is a biblical truth; don't wait until the battle is over before you praise God. Your praise may be the very thing that brings your life the deliverance and victory you need.

Praising during a struggle or victory also develops your faith. In developing your faith, praise strengthens your ability to walk in your deliverance. The bible tells us that life and death is in the power of the tongue. (Proverbs 18:21) What this scripture is telling us is that we speak the things that live or die in our lives. We can speak victory over a bad habit, which in turn speaks death to the habit in your flesh. Speak your victory, and your deliverance is an awesome addition.

One last thing to note. The bible tells us in Romans 8:37 *"we are more than a conquerors,"* I believe that the only thing "more" that a conqueror, is an overcomer. A conqueror is someone who defeats or subdues something by force or to gain a surpassing victory. An overcomer is one that comes away victorious from battle. While the difference is subtle in definition, it is astounding in revelation. To be an overcomer is to withstand an attack, to hold fast in the face of opposition. A conqueror is one that seeks out the battle and is victorious. More to this point later, but what is important to note is that you cannot control how the enemy comes, but whatever direction he comes you can overcome him. Simply praise him continually, bless the Lord at all times, and allow his praise to remain in your mouth forever. Do this and there is no limit to what God can deliver you from, or the victories that he will fight on your behalf.

Destroys Barriers Between You and God's Promises (Joshua 6: 16-20)

When I first read the account of Joshua and the children of Israel shouting and destroying the wall of Jericho, I must admit I was a bit confused. On the one hand, I figured that it was out of their obedience that God destroyed the wall. While their obedience was instrumental in the wall coming down, I was perplexed as to why God would use the shout and no other means to bring down the wall.

I am a really shy person. I know that may be hard to believe, but it is the truth. I hated public speaking or singing in front of people, or anything that required me to be put in the spotlight. I tried to avoid attention as best as I could because I hated it. I tried everything to get over my fear. I used every trick in the book. I tried looking over the crowd only to catch the eyes of someone and get nervous again. I tried imagining the crowd naked only to be nervous that they were imagining me the same way (I know it's not the most church-like thing to say, but it's the truth.) Then one day I asked a preacher friend of mine what he did to get over having to preach in front of crowds. He replied that he screamed as loud as he could before he went out and then he was fine.

Initially I thought that was possibly the dumbest thing I had ever heard but because I knew him to be an intelligent person, I asked him why he did that. He told me two reasons: The first was he figured he would make a fool of himself in private first, so if he made a fool of himself in the pulpit it wouldn't be the first time that day. The second was to break the fear barrier. He explained that he screamed to force out the spirit of fear and break his inability to let sound out of his mouth. He said that a shout either of desperation or of victory forces your spirit to awaken and move on your behalf. So I shouted and shouted and shouted, and eventually I got to a place where my shout turned to praise. My shout of praise made me more confident, not in myself, but in God's ability to move me where I needed to be. A shout of praise can bring the breakthrough you need to walk into the promise. Never allow what you won't say to keep you from your destiny.

Silences Things That Come Against You
(Psalm 8:2)

One thing that I have learned as a fact of life is that haters and enemies are a promise of God. I know that may bother the theology of some readers, but the simple truth is that if you are ever doing the right thing, you are bound to have people speaking against what you do. With that being said, sometimes your biggest hater, enemy, foe, backbiter, is you. Again I know this may seem a bit odd, but every time you speak against your ability to do what God called you to do or be what God called you to be, you hate who you are and relegate your ability to who you were. Contrarily, praise can be the encouraging you need before you act on your call.

Further, praise can silence your enemies by making them fester in their own confusion. The funniest Psalm of David is one of the most quoted. David proclaims, "I will bless the Lord at all times and his praise shall continually be in my mouth," but what is not preached was that he spoke this while pretending to be insane. (See also 1 Samuel 21) Many may not find this funny, but when I would play basketball and hear a visiting school's fans screaming at me or yelling horrible things at my team, I would instantly start smiling and singing. The louder they got, the louder I got until eventually they were so busy trying to figure out what I was singing that they became silent. After one game, a group of people came up to me and said, "It's no fun bothering you." I asked them why, they responded that, it seemed like the more they tried to bother me, the stronger my game got and the happier I seemed. Praising in the face of adversity can make your adversary grow silent and try to figure out a new tactic because their words have no effect on you. Confuse your foe into silence by praising like David. It might make you appear crazy, but it makes God appear how he is: GREAT!

Restores A Heavy Spirit (Isaiah 61:3)

"What A Friend We Have in Jesus," was one of my favorite songs to hear my grandmother sing growing up because it typically meant that she was seeking God about something that had her worried. The song is so transformative to me, but also forces you to look at the shifting of burden carrying. We are directed to lay our burdens at the feet of Jesus, but sometimes it is the journey from where we are to where He is that makes the burden seem that much heavier. Whether it is a loss of a loved one, or the return of an illness, the things that we carry not only make life seem difficult to navigate, but it places a weight on our spirit that can make it feel worse. God says in Isaiah that he gives an exchange for this spirit. For the heaviness of Zion; he gave a garment of praise. This is somewhat interesting in that the scripture does not say that he gives us a spirit of praise for a spirit of heaviness, but rather a garment or a covering. So he takes away the heavy spirit and covers us with praise.

Being engaged in praise can sometimes change a mood quicker than a word from God. Rendering praise to God can so shift the atmosphere of your heart that it pushes the corners of your mouth upright and brightens the glimmer in your eye. Wearing this garment of praise allows God to plant you as an "oak of righteousness to display His splendor." Then, God will promote a praiser to such a place where others are able to marvel at his or her ability to move, live and succeed through praise.

Pleases God (Psalm 69:30-31)

Each reason previously given is great a reason to praise God but the true sign of a mature believer is his or her ability to make God smile through praise. God loves to know that we appreciate Him. He loves to know that we care enough about Him to praise Him. Children's character Barney says that thank you is one of the magic words. Praise is our way of giving God thanks. Paul told us that in everything give thanks for this is the will of God. Give thanks, not for the benefits, but for simply His being God.

Praise in the church has become nothing more than our response to a beneficial outcome to something that God has brought us to and through, but the real truth about praise the word implores us to live out is the realization that God is worth it, even when He doesn't do what we expect him to do. Paul states in 2 Corinthians 12:7-10:

"Because of the surpassing greatness of the revelations, for this reason, to keep me from exalting myself, there was given me a thorn in the flesh, a messenger of Satan to torment me—to keep me from exalting myself! Concerning this I implored the Lord three times that it might leave me. And He has said to me, "My grace is sufficient for you, for power is perfected in weakness." Most gladly, therefore, I will rather boast about my weaknesses, so that the power of Christ may dwell in me. Therefore I am well content with weaknesses, with insults, with distresses, with persecutions, with difficulties, for Christ's sake; for when I am weak, then I am strong."

This is a revelation that we all must get. Only pride can come out of a false expectation of God and an unhealthy confidence in yourself. I received a similar revelation early on in life. For those that do not know, I was born left hand dominant. While that may not seem to be a big deal, any one that has tried to sit in a classroom with the seats that had desks attached understands exactly what my issue was. I never fully understood it honestly. I couldn't write without smudging my paper which made some interesting conversations with my teacher about how my hand erased all my work. That excuse never worked by the way. And I just hated it so I taught myself, at the cost of my penmanship, to write with my right hand. Eventually I figured it out and was excited that I was like everyone else. That is until I started playing sports. I never understood why I was shooting and throwing and doing anything remotely athletic with my left hand. I worked hard and tried to be a better player with my right and although my right was good it was never as good as my left hand. I began to hate that I was left handed. That is until I got to high school. The summer before I started school I was in a basketball camp and my eventual coach saw me shooting and ran over and said, "Don't tell me you are left handed?" I shrugged my shoulders and said I guess. He smiled and excitedly yelled and said to the assistant coaches, "We have a left hand shooter, a new deadly weapon!" What I saw as dysfunction, he saw as my greatest gift.

Paul like me looked at his "thorn" as a frailty, a mark in his armor. He wanted God to remove the issue from him so badly that he kept going to Him in prayer about it. God's reply that His "grace is sufficient" said to Paul what we all should now understand and that is that God's strength can cover us in our weakness. That in spite of the circumstance or flaw, God can show Himself strong in it, without removing the problem. Our issues allow us to see, know and understand more of who and what God is, and if that isn't reason enough to praise God in your troubles, I don't know what is!

WORSHIP AS A WITNESS

I once asked a few people what was the one thing I did and said that absolutely got on their last nerve. Now before I go into it, I really believe that this is something that everyone should do at some point. Friends tend to be nice at times and would rather shield you from being hurt then to tell you the truth. But don't ask if you REALLY don't want to know the answer. In surveying my friends the unanimous answer was a phrase that unfortunately for them and fortunately for me, I still use to this day: "That's Funny!" Now this may seem like it should not bother anyone. It's only two words and not irritating or offensive. Well for me, that phrase is my way of describing anything. If I hear a funny joke, I say it. If someone does something that lacks a certain level of intelligence for their age (yes that is my nice way of saying someone did something stupid), I say it. That phrase could follow up any and everything without saying anything at the same time. While it means a slew of things to me, it means completely nothing to my friends. In this we find the same separation between our understanding of praise and worship.

Praise is easily identifiable. Whether that praise is authentic or not, you can always tell when praise is going forth. That is not to say that you can tell why a person is a praising, but the act of praise goes well beyond the four walls of the church. There is a kind of praise in every aspect of life. When a child uses the potty for the first time you applaud and tell them how good he or she did. When a student gets an "A" in school, you tell her how proud of her you are. When you go to work and finish a big project, your boss gives you a bonus to show his appreciation. You may even want to applaud after you read this and might be amazed at the fact that I made a potty training reference in a spiritual book.

Worship in the modern church, however, seems to be a bit more elusive. Worship is used to describe everything and nothing at the same time. Our services are worship services, our tithing is an act of worship, and our songs are worship songs. To a degree this is true. Everything that we do, or rather should do, can be defined as worship, but in the context the church has used it discredits or diminishes the value of what worship truly is. If this is the case, then there are two possibilities: either there is something that binds all of these things into the very thing that is worship, or the church is wrong for categorizing everything as worship. The simple answer to this question is both possibilities are correct. Worship is a part of everything we do as believers, and yet it is not everything that we do as believers. I know that concept seems a bit difficult to understand, but I promise it will make sense.

To break down the many uses in the bible and exegesis every single grouping within it would be a book of its own. So before I go any further, please do not take this chapter to define what worship is. More importantly, it is an attempt to get you to understand two concepts: what it does and what is needed for it to be true.

As I said previously, I love cars, but I have not always been a car-savvy person. I once used to drive a Chevy Lumina. I thought that car was the greatest car on earth. I mean, for a person that didn't have access to much, it was perfect for me. Not because of the style of the car, not because of the sleek interior, but simply because it worked. I rarely had to worry about the car. One summer day, I went out to drive to the store and the car did not start. I was so frustrated, flustered, and honestly a bit irritated. I thought the only time that the car would not work would be because of cold weather or something like that, but this beautiful summer day the car chose not to start. I began to panic a bit, called my parents and told them that the car was not working anymore. My grandfather just happened to be visiting us from Detroit, and he overheard me talking and decided to chime in on the conversation. He asked me, what sound does the car make? Did it turn over? Was there oil on the ground? Was there smoke under the engine? After answering all of those questions my grandfather told me to try to start the car. I fussed at him because it was not going to start, but to appease him I went back outside and turned the key in the ignition. Again the car did not start. Then my grandfather looked at me and laughed. I did not think anything was funny so I asked him why he was laughing. He said, "Did you really think the car would start without gas in it!" I was a bit embarrassed. I told him I knew the gas light was on, but I didn't think the car wouldn't start if it got me home the last time I drove it.

For many of us, we ignore the warning signs that we are missing the "gas in our car." Faith, love, hope and belief, are all awesome things to experience with respect to people, but worship is the only way they can be experienced with respect to God. It is in worship that we develop our relationship and interaction with God. Worship is the very thing that fuels all that we live by. Some of us try and do what I did with the car. We try and make it as long as we can off our last worship encounter not realizing we are running on fumes and when God calls us to act, we are unable because we have not worshiped since Sunday. That in turn renders us unable to hear the call or act uninhibited by the things around you. Would you try to make it all week on one gallon of gas in a car that you drive all day every day? Of course, not!

Some of us move into and through so many trials that we find ourselves on empty by Sunday night, even though we were filled up Sunday morning. It's interesting to see so many of us lost in what we consider worship, but never notice the lack of change around us. We build churches and other edifices, we grow in numbers, but we fail to make an impact on anything around us because we don't have the fuel needed to change our community. A car without fuel cannot go anywhere! No matter how fancy or expensive it is, or how much we maintain the parts, or how much we spend on accessories, it cannot and will not move. Worship empowers us to act. Not just act, but to initiate change in our surroundings. In worship we allow ourselves to be so connected to God that the change and movement that He sees, we become.

Some may read this and say that I am overstating the importance of worship. They will argue that it is faith that moves us and faith that powers all that we do. Well let's examine the two and begin to dissect what worship is to us. Hebrews 11:1 says, *"...faith is the substance of things hoped for and the evidence of things not seen."* With this understanding, we know that according to Hebrews 11:6, it is impossible to please God without faith. It is for this reason that I stated previously that faith is the keys to our spiritual car. It is the thing that gives us access; it is the thing that allows everything else to function, but with that being said if you start a car without gas (as I tried to do) you will see that it will go nowhere. So what exactly is this fuel? What exactly is the thing that gives power? Well the simple answer is the Holy Spirit and our use of it through worship. For those that are deep, let me explain this further. Worship is our way of connecting to the power of God in such a way that it empowers us to move in the things of God. It is an acknowledgement of our frailty through adoration of an omnipotent God. It is how we are acknowledged by God.

In Matthew 7:22-23 Jesus says, *"On that day many will say to me, 'Lord, Lord, did we not prophesy in your name, and cast out demons in your name, and do many deeds of power in your name?* ^{23} *Then I will declare to them, 'I never knew you; go away from me, you evildoers.'"* Now looking at the scripture you can notice two things beyond the fact that Jesus is speaking pretty emphatically given the bold letters. The first is that those that are rejected are performing, but do not have access. They apparently have operated in the gifts of the spirit, moving in what they thought to be purpose, and doing it all in the power of the Name above all Names, and yet Jesus does not receive them. Many people are operating in gift and not relationship. You have power because of the gift, and you affect change in the people that you are connected to and are accepted for your gift, but not accepted by God. What has become of the church when we are okay with gifts but not power? What has become of the people of God when we accept change without power, movement without the Spirit, results without relationship?

Faith says that we can move into the unseeable when we can obtain what we cannot comprehend. Worship allows the unseeable to move through us, the incomprehensible to obtain and grab hold of us! Which begs the second thing to point out in this scripture: everyone who came to Jesus knew who he was, but Jesus did not know them. I remember as a kid I use to love going to play basketball at different gyms. There was one specific gym that I loved to go to, not because of the facilities but because of the gym's manager. I am from Chicago, and there was another native Chicagoan that had the same last name as me, Quinn Buckner. He was a famous basketball player and apparently he was the gym manager's favorite player. So whenever I came to the gym, he would clear out one of the rims for me so I could practice on my game. One summer to my dismay, the gym manager didn't clear out the rim for me and actually was acting a bit rude to me. So when I asked him what was wrong he told me that he met Quinn at a charity event and when he asked him about me, he had no clue that I was. I was receiving privileges for a connection that I did not have. Many people today are given privileges and gaining access into places they have no real right to and are operating as if they do. A Christian is not a person that knows Jesus, but a person that Jesus knows. Anyone can know the name of Jesus, but how many of us can say that Jesus knows our name. Before I go any further let me be clear on this point God is omniscient and aware of every living thing on this earth, but for God to know you means you are in covenant with Him. In the same way, you know people at your job, but they don't have the same rights and privileges as your true friends, or better yet your spouse. Knowing God requires intimacy with God, and that is only experienced in worship.

Very specifically, worship allows God to move in, on and through you. It moves your will to the side and allows the Holy Spirit to act on your behalf. Now, it takes faith to get this "fuel" and to allow the Holy Spirit to fill you, but worship gives you access to the Holy Spirit, through intimacy.

So what do we need for worship? What is required of us to create an atmosphere that is conducive to pure worship with God? Genesis 22 presents the familiar story of Abraham going to sacrifice his son Isaac. We pay a lot of attention, and rightfully so, to the image of Abraham's faith and obedience at work. Let's look at this scripture from another angle. In verse 5, Abraham tells his servants to stay at the bottom of the mountain while he and Isaac go "to worship." From this we can ascertain that from the perspective of Isaac and the servants, all they were going to do was worship. With this in mind, let's pay closer attention to Isaac's question in verse 7. Isaac, being knowledgeable of the act of worship asked Abraham, *"Behold the fire and the wood, but where is the lamb for the burnt offering?"* From Isaac's question we can now see that there are three things required for worship; fire, wood and an offering.

Fire is the simplest to understand and will be discussed at length in this chapter. Fire represents the presence of God. It represents the spirit of God's active participation in the act of worship. Fire is what consumes the entirety of the wood and the offering, such that everything that it touches is affected and structurally changed because of it. This fire can only come from God and as such should never go out. (see Leviticus 6:12-13) It is in this that we fully understand that *"if any man be in Christ, he is a new creation; the old has gone, the new has come!"* (2 Corinthians 5:17) The consuming fire of God is what changes our makeup and transforms us into what God requires. We encounter this fire through worship.

The wood is representative of the altar. To better understand the purposes of the altar, think of it as a collage. A collage is a composition of items (pictures, drawings, cloth, etc.) affixed together to create a singular image. In a collage we often give focus to the individual pictures, but often the creator had a singular idea or stream of thought in mind when they created it. Such is the case for the altar of our testimony. Let me try and make this easy to understand. Wood is a very generic and yet specific word. If you burn wood from an oak tree, the scent of that would be different than the wood from a cherry tree or a rubber tree. Each piece of wood has its identifying marks, traits, and its own scent when burned. Your testimony is the same way. Each trial that we face in life adds to the identity of our altar. Further, it is the testimonies before, after and during our trials that help us create the place where we give our sacrifice of worship. There is line in the song "My Worship Is For Real" by Bishop Larry Trotter that says, "You can't feel my pain, what I had to go through to get here." The way we address God in the act of worship is specific to not only how we met God, but how we continue to see God through our trials. The wood of worship is what intermingles with the sacrifice that gives off a specific "soothing aroma" to God that determines our response from God.

While the scripture speaks specifically of "wood," please know what we build our altar with will always represent the broken nature of our struggle. We are identified by our struggle and we all have a different identifying issue. When you think of Christ, one of the things that often comes across the mind of the Christian is the cross. We identify the cross as the place of Christ's sacrifice and it was something that he had to endure. He goes on to identify us with the same thing in Luke 9:23 when Jesus says, *"If anyone wishes to come after Me, he must deny himself, and take up his cross daily and follow me."* Our cross is our burden to bear that is specific to us in that Jesus states clearly that a follower must take up "his cross." That cross, our altar, was premade by God as the place where we too must encounter our daily sacrifice.

In a Wendy's commercial 1984, three elderly ladies walk into a fast food restaurant called Fluffy Bun and are greeted with a hamburger. Two of the women exchange commentary on the bun of the burger saying things like "that sure is a big fluffy bun." As they exchange comments, the third woman yells in disgust, at seeing the miniscule burger patty in the middle of the bun, "Where's the beef?" Having a cross to bear is unavoidable, and the presence of God is something that only God himself can reveal and give to us, but the true place of departure for many of us is the same question that Isaac asks, "Where is the sacrifice?" As in the commercial, we make comments about how a person's life appears to look, and how big a church is or how much money the church or the pastor has to make. In asking those questions, we often ignore the apparent lack of the sacrifice. We can pile up our testimonies a mile high and create the greatest altar known to man. We can request the presence of God with the greatest gut-wrenching fervor, but none of it means anything without the sacrifice. Worship is empty without a sacrifice. In Romans 12:1, Paul says we are to *"present our bodies as a living sacrifice, holy and pleasing to God this is your spiritual act of worship"* (or reasonable service in the KJV). Simply put, you are the sacrifice. The thing that is needed to conduct true worship is a life, a heart, a mind and a soul completely intent on being used and consumed by the fire of God as presented on the altar of our testimony.

The next issue to deal with is now that we know what worship does and what we need, now we must address what makes it real. Fortunately, this is a question that Jesus deals with directly. In John 4, Jesus speaks to a woman at the well. During the conversation, the woman said:

"Our fathers worshipped in this mountain, and you people say that in Jerusalem is the place where men ought to worship." Jesus replied by saying "Woman, believe Me, an hour is coming when neither in this mountain nor in Jerusalem will you worship the Father. You worship what you do not know; we worship what we know, for salvation, is from the Jews. But an hour is coming and now is, when the true worshipers will worship the Father in spirit and truth, for such people the Father seeks to be His worshipers. God is spirit, and those who

worship Him must worship in spirit and truth."

Now for a simple reader like myself, there is a lot to digest in this small conversation, but let me try and point out a few things. First, true worship is not relegated to a physical place. I know that we like to call the church a worship center, but the truth is that the building was called to be a "house of prayer," according to Matthew 21:13, not a house of worship. Now this is not to say that the church house is not a place for worship or worshipers, but rather that it is not the only place for worship.

The next comment of Jesus is a description of two types of worship: Spirit-led worship and truth-led worship. Now I can fully develop both concepts in depth, but let's make the understanding of these concepts a bit simpler. The word in this scripture for spirit literally means the spirit of God. Now we can dissect what that really means and its applicability to us in the church, but let me make this very clear and very easy: worship free from God is not worship. When you think of the NBA's Chicago Bulls, who is the first person that comes to mind? My favorite player is Scottie Pippen but even I think Michael Jordan when I think of the Bulls. Nothing you do can separate Jordan from the legacy of the Bulls. You can love another player; you can enjoy the current team. The team could win a championship and everything that happens after will always find its way back to include Jordan. In that same way, nothing should ever separate your worship from God. You can enjoy the song and the singer. You can appreciate the moment, but true worship requires the presence of the spirit of God flowing through the worshipper. You can praise something that is not a part of you, but worship requires the worshipper and the object of their worship to be conjoined such that you cannot separate them from one another.

In order for this to happen, you have to separate yourself from more than just the physical space you are in, but rather you have to be receptive to all things that could hold you back from being a part of the intimate moment. It is at this place that we meet the next part of worship that God seeks: a place of truth. Truth in this text means what is true in any manner under consideration and purity of mind which is free from affection, pretense, simulation, falsehood and deceit. To keep the theme of allowing this to remain simple, what we need to take from this is that all barriers that prevent us from allowing God to move, must be removed. All concerns, cares and burdens; all presumptions and expectations must be laid to the side and all of your focus, hope and belief have to be set on God, the apprehension of his presence and the intimacy of his spirit. Truth, in the context of worship, says that at that moment, at that second, nothing else matters, nothing else can be on your mind other than God.

It is ironic how currently we are searching for alternative fuels sources. The price of gas is astronomical. It is becoming harder and harder to sustain our rate of current use and so we substitute battery cells, or other more "natural" fuel sources for gas. What makes this even more interesting is that the fuel in the vehicle is predetermined before the vehicle is used. A car that takes gas can't run on corn oil. A battery-operated vehicle has no use for gasoline. The state of the believer and the church is that we are accepting different fuels than the fuel we were created to use, which is worship. We were created to give and immerse ourselves in worship, and this interaction with God is what fuels our ability to move in the things of God. Without clear, intimate worship, a song will only be a song, a service only a service. The people of God need to come back to the heart of worship, which makes worship all and only about our God.

I GOT TEN ON IT: TITHING & OFFERING

Farming is a very interesting profession. Unlike most professions, it is solely affected by naturally uncontrollable, yet somewhat predictable occurrences. If you don't plant at the right time, if you get too much rain or too much sun, or if you harvest the produce too soon you will miss any opportunity to use that which you have worked hard to grow. Despite all the work, consideration and attention that is required to farm, there is still an abundance of farmers. Furthermore, even with the unpredictable climate and the condition of the grounds because of it, every season farmers still go out and plant again in anticipation of the next harvest.

In the Christian faith, we too are called to be farmers, but of a different kind. Each of us is called to plant different types of seed, and some seeds take root more easily than others. We are called to sow encouragement, love, peace and joy into the lives of others. We are also called to sow the most precious seed of all in others, the seed of the gospel of Christ. And still there is another seed that tends to draw the ire and angst of the people: money! Specifically I am talking about the struggle the church has with tithing.

Over the years, sermons about tithing have become so rare that some preachers and pastors steer clear of the subject completely. People leave churches, and congregations draw silent whenever the subject of a tithe or offering is brought up. What may be misunderstood in the debates about the tithe are three basic things: 1) the need for the tithe, 2) the blessing of the tithe and 3) the relation of the tithe to the rest of our giving and worship.

The Need

You know, I always understood how government works. I knew that it was through taxes and several other forms of funding and borrowing that allows everything in our country to run. Sometimes government chooses to run slower than normal, but we must pay for everything that we have. Unfortunately, your participation in the process is never voluntary. Whether you like it or not, somehow, someway you are paying into the system. You buy groceries which are taxed. You work a job and get a check that is taxed. You buy a house and pay property taxes. There is no escaping paying into the system. Thankfully the kingdom of God does not operate like that. While God requires your sacrifice and God requires your diligence, he does not force the issue. As it relates to your tithe, we have all read the scriptures and understand that tithing is a spiritual request from God, not a natural mandate from your pastor or your church. Tithing is like one of those things that you don't really understand how much it's needed until it's not there.

Now let me clear up some of the misconceptions people have. The first is that the church does not need the tithe. With pastors, preachers sporting brand new cars and new houses while congregations around the country struggle in this economy, I understand why you would think the church does not need your tithe, but let me help you look at it another way. Most people that carry this sentiment believe that it is the church to which we are tithing, but the truth is we are thinking of the tithe in a very limited way. The church, as defined by God, is comprised of us all, myself included. We are not only the body of Christ we are also the bride of Christ. As a result, the church needs each part of "the body" in working order. Now that you understand the church, let me help you understand why the church needs your tithe. It has very little to do with the money. Any person who makes it about the money is missing the point, because it is more about what the tithe represents. The tithe represents not just obedience, but an understanding of where we are with God. It represents our ability to say to God that we are fully invested in what he is doing. I have heard that we need to give the three T's: tithe, talent and time. Well, do not separate the group and you will have a clearer view of what God is requesting. A singer that has not submitted to God is just a great vocalist. A preacher who is not dedicated to God can speak and inspire, but could never do so with the power of Christ. You can spend all day in the church, but if you are not committed to the purposes of God for your life and striving to submit to his will, then you are just wasting your time. A person who tithes has to think the same way. Our commitment is measured by our willingness to sacrifice for the greater good of the whole "body".

Once I severely broke my toe. It was so bad that I had to wear a boot on my foot. Now that may not sound bad, but try wearing an open toe boot in the middle of a Chicago winter. Not painful enough to you yet? Well try walking around downtown Chicago in the middle of winter every day for three months! It had to be one of my worst injuries simply because of how it affected my ability to do everything else. At the time it happened my thought was, "It is only a toe I will be fine!" However, as each day came and went, I knew that such a small injury can change EVERYTHING! Finally it healed and I was able to take the boot off. I get to church and prepare to sing with the praise team when someone ask me, "Why aren't you wearing your boot?" I said it had healed and she responded, "But you are still walking with a limp." I realized that she was right. My body had gotten used to walking with the injury and I had to train it to walk without the limp I developed while I did not have full use of my toe.

Some of us look at the tithe as I looked at my toe. We think that if we take care of everything else, then our tithe is just an insignificant piece of a greater puzzle that God intended. As a result, the church has been forced to "limp along" without it. We need the body in full working order and that requires the sacrifice of the whole person, which includes the tithe. Comedians make jokes about the many "funds" that the church now employs. We have a building fund, Africa fund, a fund to do evangelism, a fund to feed the needy, a fund to even help church members to believe. It is my belief that if the body was fully functioning in the things of God through the tithe, we would have the ability to meet every need in the house!

The Blessing

To give out of pure routine is misguided giving. The main point of what the tithe represents speaks to the faith of a tither. As with the farmer, a ground without seed cannot produce. Faith is the seed we are giving when we tithe. We are saying to God, "Thank you for the harvest. Now I sow back into you a portion of that harvest so that you can produce more. Not just for me, but for everyone and everything you need." So in essence the tithe is not simply a sowing of money, but rather a sowing of your faith and speaks to your commitment to God's greater plan. You never tithe to a building; you tithe to God. Now with that being said, the health of a ministry is determined by the commitment of the people within the ministry. As a result, the church, for its health, needs us to go above and beyond the tithe. In the early church, as described throughout the first few chapters of Acts, the crowds were so committed to the cause of the ministry that they sold everything and relied upon each other to live. Specifically, Acts 2:44-47 shows that all believers, not just the apostles but all believers *"were together and had everything in common."* What this scripture goes on to say is that they did whatever was needed to meet a need within the group. The modern church has a long way to go in returning to this type of commitment to the cause and communal living, but it is my belief and prayer that the tithe will stop being just a conversation in the church as believers be moved to give it all for God! Some people will want to sweep this notion under a rug as a cultural divide, but the truth of scripture is that we cannot move together without agreement (Amos 3:3). Agreement goes beyond a spoken bond to a unity of mind, heart and spirit.

The simplest way to explain the blessing of the tithe relates to what you are showing God and what, in turn, he will show to you. As stated previously, the tithe is a sign of faith. It is this kind of faith that opens the door for God to move into the area of faith you are exercising. Think of it this way: There is a commercial for a product that shows two parents talking and their children are playing soccer. There is a bunch of children running and playing, but there are a few children that are sluggish. Not only are they sluggish, but one is in a french fry costume and another is shaped like a donut. The point of this commercial is to say that whatever you put into your body, you get out of it. God's kingdom works similarly. You can run around and exercise, but if you are not feeding your faith and exercising it properly, then what you don't do will catch up with you. Every area of your life requires that you exercise faith in it. Your friendship, your relationships, even understanding yourself takes different types of effort and energy. The more we seek to do in the body of Christ, the more we have to be willing to become available to the moves of God by giving him access and control over that area. As we bless God through our giving, it opens up the possibility for God to bless others, including you!

The Tie That Binds

The truth is that most people are hesitant to tithe, because we are asked to give toward many other things like the building fund, first family fund, new building fund, Africa, the place down the street, India; it all can become a bit much. This is where we must understand the single truth that binds them all and that is covenant. In a family, a child never is concerned with much of anything. If the parents have it, then the children have it. Taking it a step further, the wife as well as the husband understands that although we have individual wants, the needs of the whole should always supersede the agenda of the individual (at least, family at its best works this way). Such is the case within God's kingdom. As long as we operate as cell groups striving to change the world one section at a time, while pushing our individual agenda and not the purpose of our faith collectively, then we are destined to fail. It is the place of the covenant that we extend our commitment to the total need and not just the immediate need. Using the example of the family, a diligent parent prepares for a child's education. You put money away and you save up toward the child's future. While you spend to meet the immediate need (food, clothing shelter, entertainment, etc.), you also prepare for what is to come. You do not stop to think while saving for your child's future, "Well what if they never graduate from high school," or, "I mean they don't really need to eat today. They ate three times yesterday."

I remember the first time my mother let me take care of my brothers for a week. I can think of fewer moments when revelation came so quickly in life. It takes a lot of thought and effort to take care of somebody. You have to be at work and think about dinner, activities so they don't get bored etc. When the time comes you have to do all this stuff, you are exhausted from just thinking about it. Because I love my brothers and I didn't want to let my parents down, I did whatever I needed to do to make sure that they were okay. For anyone who has a child, especially a boy who eats like a human garbage can, God bless your ministry. My brothers spent the day eating everything and would then ask, "What are we eating for dinner?" The first day we just ate out. I figured it was only a week and I'm at work all day so I only really have to worry about dinner. How wrong I was. I learned very quickly that growing children only think about three things: food, recreation and sleep. By the end of the week I felt broke, tired and frustrated. I felt like all I did was feed, give and after giving they asked me to give some more. Now I know that my experience only lasted a week, but I learned very quickly that no matter how much I gave, I continued to find more ways to give. Yes, it was frustrating I did not want to do so much all the time, but my heart would not allow me to withhold what they needed and what they wanted as I was led. Just as my parents have done with me, God has done something similar with us. God has entrusted his people, in our hands to care for. Caring for His church means preparing it for his coming, and this has costs. It costs in time, in talents and in tithes and offering. Giving is our way of saying that we are invested in the covenant. It says that we choose to bind ourselves to what the church needs. Just as I fed my brothers, we have to feed God's people. And it is not just about money. The bible says that, "*Where your treasure is, there your heart will be also.*"(Matthew 6:21) What this is saying is where we place value is where we place ourselves. If I did not love my brothers, I would have left them in the house alone to fend for themselves. Their well-being would not be my concern and I would rationalize why they are not my responsibility. By placing your tithe in the hands of God through the church, you show that you are fully invested in the purpose of God for this generation and generations to come.

If we truly care about the world God has entrusted into our hands, let's do what it takes to show God that he left it all in capable hands. You give and tithe to secure the future and the present state of a thing. Meet the need and secure the future with your tithe!

THE DEVIL MADE ME DO IT: SIN

I grew up in a family where at one point or another everything was sin. This is not an exaggeration. I am not just talking about the big stuff either like lying, stealing etc., but everything. Stayed out too long? You are sinning. Watching music videos? That's a sin. Tight clothes on? Sin. Women with pants on, that would send you to hell with gasoline underwear on in a wooden basket. Everything and anything was considered sin.

Before you read this chapter any further, please understand that this is not an attempt to define exactly what does and does not qualify as sin. Even Paul in pointing out the evident sins in Galatians 5 does not give an exhaustive list. The reason this is of no consequence is because there are two things that we need to understand. First is a simple concept that does not require much explanation. That concept is that everybody has sinned. I am not being presumptuous when I say this either. Paul says it also in Romans 3:23. This is important to understand because no one is exempt from needing repentance. We all, in one way or another, struggle with sin or the temptation to sin. The nature of sin is simply the nature of flesh; no matter how hard you try, it will always be there. Paul, in Romans 7 talks about how sin and the flesh always try to trip you up, and as long as you are in the flesh you a susceptible to sin.

Now that I have successfully discouraged your attempt to run away from sin, let me give you the second thing that you must understand: it is possible to live above sin. I once had a conversation with a preacher who was trying to get me to understand sin. After a long conversation that went pretty much nowhere because of my many questions, he asked me, "Do you think it is possible for a person not to sin?" I told him yes! He replied, "Then you are delusional." To which I replied, "Then the bible is fake." In Leviticus 11:44 God said to *"be holy for I am holy."* Luke 6:40 says that everyone that is perfect will be like his master. What this preacher did not understand, and I did not understand fully, is that while not one of us is God, we are all called to be like God, and that is separated and free from sin. What both of these scriptures and many others speak to is our ability to allow God to keep us. Paul asked in 2 Corinthians 6:14, *"What fellowship does righteousness have with lawlessness and darkness have with light?"* What this rhetorical question is posing to us is how we as the church can and should be different. There is a huge difference between a person who falls into sin and a person who is a sinner. The primary difference being, one makes a mistake, and the other believes that what they have done is not wrong. Stumbling is one thing, but acceptance of failure is just plain unacceptable.

If you've been paying attention, you know that I loved basketball when I was growing up. Every year I tried to get better and better at every aspect of the game. In eighth grade I was about five-feet and seven inches which meant I had to work even harder to be good. One day during a lay-up line my coach yelled out, "Hey Buckner, whenever you want to jump we will be ready!" Apparently he was making a joke about the fact that I could not jump high at all. I had friends my height that could touch the backboard and I was stuck trying to slap the net. I got so frustrated with this that I worked diligently to be a better jumper. Eventually my net-slapping turned into backboard-slapping, which turned into rim-grabbing which turned into dunks. At any point I could have settled, but I was determined to be my best in that area. So too is the difference between someone that makes a mistake and a sinner. Sinners settle. Instead of trying to be better, they make excuses as to why they can't do what they should. Instead of aspiring to dunk, they say I am only this tall so I can't reach the rim. A person who makes a mistake lives daily in an attempt to attain what began in their eyes as impossible. At that height, there was no way on Earth I believed it was normal for me to dunk, but I never let go of the thought that I could. Instead of fighting lust a sinner says, we all have sinned and nobody is perfect. A person that makes a mistake says in that same situation I know this is hard and I know I want to, but I can do and be what God says.

Now that I have gotten that out of the way, let me explain the true reason for this chapter: Flip Wilson. Flip Wilson is a comedian who at the height of his career in the 1970s was well known for a female character he played named Geraldine. Geraldine was the typical African American exaggerated female character who constantly got into a little bit more trouble than she should have. Whenever she would do something disagreeable, she made the statement that became a national and international craze: "The devil made me do it." No matter what it was that happened, somehow the devil would step in and force her to do it. Whether it was driving a car into a church, or buying a dress that she should not have, every time anything happened, the devil made her do it. This too has become the state of the church. We have gotten into a routine where we believe everything that happens in life to throw us off course is because of the devil. A family member gets sick, the devil got her. Someone dies unexpectedly, the devil did it. The church has become so preoccupied with the devil that we have deprioritized the work and movements of God. These three things are required to understand sin and our response and role in it: First, spiritual warfare begins and ends with you. Second, it is ridiculous to run from a defeated foe (a quipped quote from Bishop Noel Jones). Finally, you must come to realize that sin has no levels.

Sin City

It's funny to me whenever I hear about movies made in or family and friends who have taken a trip to Las Vegas. Everyone comes back and says how the city can just take hold of you, and you find yourself up all night and doing things that are just unspeakable, but it is ok because "what happens in Vegas stays in Vegas." Afraid of ever being overtaken by the city, for years I refused to go. Then I had a very interesting conversation with a friend who I knew was more saved than me. He had decided to go to Vegas with some family and just hang out. When he got back, I asked him if we had to have a deliverance service just for him to get that Vegas spirit out of him. He said something that I did not expect. He said, "Honestly bro, Vegas is super boring!" Shocked, I asked if he was just feeding me part of the "what happens in Vegas..." mantra. He said, "No, Vegas has its cool sites, some really nice architecture and can be a lot of fun, but if you aren't drinking, gambling and staying up all night then there isn't much else to do."

Unlike my friend, most people take this same approach to sin and spiritual warfare. We insist that it is the presence of evil that causes us to sin and that we just cannot help ourselves. The truth is that every sin we commit, YES EVERY SIN, can be defined by a choice; a choice to decide between what our flesh desires and what our spirit requires. Before I go any further, I do not deny the existence of evil spirits and our need to fight them at every turn, but what I am saying is that an individual has a choice to follow the flesh or the spirit. James 1 gives us a clear understanding of how sin comes. In verses 14 and 15 James says, "but each person is tempted when they are dragged away by their own evil desires and enticed. Then, after desire has conceived, it gives birth to sin; and sin when it is full-grown, gives birth to death." What James establishes is a clear relationship between what we want and what we do. As stated in verse 13, God does not tempt us, but rather it is our own desires that allow us to be tempted.

Now at this point is when most people talk to me about the armor of God and our role in the fight against the enemy. Well let's take a look at that armor.

"Finally, be strong in the Lord and in his mighty power. Put on the full armor of God, so that you can take your stand against the devil's schemes. For our struggle is not against flesh and blood, but against the rulers, against the authorities, against the powers of this dark world and against the spiritual forces of evil in the heavenly realms. Therefore, put on the full armor of God, so that when the day of evil comes, you may be able to stand your ground and after you have done everything, to stand. Stand firm then, with the belt of truth buckled around your waist, with the breastplate of righteousness in place, and with your feet fitted with the readiness that comes from the gospel of peace. In addition to all this, take up the shield of faith, with which you can extinguish all the flaming arrows of the evil one. Take the helmet of salvation and the sword of the Spirit, which is the word of God. And pray in the Spirit on all occasions with all kinds of prayers and requests. With this in mind, be alert and always keep on praying for all the Lord's people." (Ephesians 6:10-18)

The essential characteristics of this depiction of the Christian is key to the belief that the devil can get to us and make us react, respond or destroyed as a result of a battle lost to him and his many demons, but look closely first at the armor. A soldier wears armor not to fight but to be protected during the fight. In that manner, so too are we to wear this armor of God… not to fight the enemy, but rather to be prepared to remove yourself from harm during the attacks of the enemy. Now instead of pulling out the armor, look at what the armor represents: Truth, righteousness, gospel of peace, faith, salvation and the word of God. If we are honest, these are the basic requirements to being a disciple of Christ and inevitably, a Christian. Taking up the armor of God does not allow you to fight sin, but rather it allows you to resist sin and the enemy and watch them both flee from you. The sin you constantly face is the sin you have not submitted to God (James 4:7-10) or have not learned to accept the grace of God in that space to push you into being better (2 Corinthians 12:6-10).

Knockout

Let me ask you a question. What happened when Lucifer was cast out of heaven? Here's a better question, what happened when Christ ascended into heaven? Got one more for you. If Christ is coming back to reclaim the world, what happens to the devil? I once heard a sermon where someone said the devil is defeated and then 10 minutes later the same person said we have to war against the devil. To me that begged the question how can God defeat something that we are struggling to fight? The simple truth is we are fighting a battle we have no business fighting. Now before I go any further let me not confuse you by saying again that spiritual warfare is real, but it is a fight where by the fighter, is more important than the tool.

Boxing is different from most sports in that you don't necessarily have to fight an opponent that you have beaten. Whether it is a close fight or not often the choice for a rematch is left to the champion. Too often we give our enemies rematches, and as a result, we fall into sin. Remember the concept of desire. Throughout your life if every struggle that you faced is the same that truly means that it is a struggle that you have failed to defeat decisively, but by defeating that struggle, that enemy, that sin, you must not forget the occurrence of the battle. Sin comes in many forms. As our desires change, so does the way we are tempted, which means so does the sin we are susceptible to, but if we are content with fighting the same fights then we lose sight of what we are called to be, which is an overcomer.

Overcomer v. Conqueror

Have you ever looked at your life and truly considered how you got where you are? Have you ever considered the truth of your circumstance? I have often asked myself this very question, but I have never been forced to ask it as much as I have been over the course of the last few years. Through various trials and tests, I have come to several conclusions that I believe believers must come to at some point in their walk.

First, you are either a product of your environment or your environment is a product of you! People often tend to reject the idea that their surroundings are a direct reflection of either their own reality or the truth of their life. For example, typically when people are in a dark place or a dry place they wear dark-colored clothes, stay in seclusion and often talk to people who are in a similar place in life. I wish I could say that the life of the believer is different, but too often we all fall into this trap of allowing our emotional state to dictate our physical state. I know that when I feel confused or lost, my room gets messy, my study notes get scattered, and I literally lose everything. It's even hard for me to keep up with the days of the week! Taking it a step further, when I feel hurt I tend to gravitate toward either people I know that are hurting or (sadly enough) people who have hurt me in the past. When I do this, I'm allowing the hurt to overpower any feeling of God, it in turn feeds and grows off the negativity of others.

There are also times when I allow the negativity of others to turn my cheerful and happy demeanor into a self-deprecating festival. I have learned that it only makes sense for people to gravitate to where they perceive themselves to be. If you never confront the issue of seeing the flaws in you, then you will never be willing to change your environment.

Light and darkness cannot be one and the same. Even from the foundations of the Earth, God meant for there to be a separation between light and darkness. Genesis 1:4 says *"And God saw the light, that it was good: and God DIVIDED the light from the darkness."* Anyone that lives according to the light (the Spirit of God) cannot dwell in places of darkness because it becomes uncomfortable. That is because God ordained for there to be a separation of the two. Paul said in 2 Corinthians 6:14, "*Be not unequally yoked together with unbelievers: for what fellowship hath righteousness and unrighteousness? And what communion hath light with darkness?*" You can't be a person of faith and be committed to a person without faith. One of the two will win out; either the other person will change or you will change. Bishop Noel Jones says to the believer, "If you can't change the people around you, change the people around you!" If you cannot bring growth to those who are around you, and they are not doing the same for you, there is a need for you to get around people who can.

Some of us have gone through seasons where the devil has just run all over our lives. Typically it happens in times where God has allowed us to go through a season of hardship. For me, that season came with the loss of my grandmother. Before she passed, I was in the middle of learning how to walk with God. I was truly a babe in Christ, and when stuff got hard I leaned on my grandmother. After she passed, I lost my way in a major way. I lost all interest in school, and my grades dropped dramatically. I walked away from all my friends and began to throw away everything I had learned up to that point. I began drinking heavily, I was staying out late and worst of all I transferred all my hurt onto the most important person in my life at the time. I was a liar, a cheater, a manipulator and so much more. I picked up so many bad habits it was not even funny. During this period, I attached myself to people who I thought would be good for the "new me." They said they went to church, but lived just as foul a life as I did. They encouraged me to stay in my state of hurt and pain. I must stop here to say, PLEASE be careful who you attach yourself to while you are in pain. Although they may do a lot of "things" for you like cook, clean, wash your clothes, etc… if they are not challenging your way of thinking and your way of living and allow you to be comfortable in your sin, then they are probably not supposed to be in your life. Proverbs 27:17 says, "*Iron sharpens iron, so a man sharpens the countenance of his friend.*" Do I fault any of the people that helped me destroy my life, NOT AT ALL! God allowed me to destroy myself just so He could be the only one to get the credit for restoring me. My loneliness is what led to my destructive relationships. What's so funny is that people were telling me that I needed to walk away and that I needed to get closer to God, but I thought that I needed the presence of another person to make me happy, or to bring me some semblance of peace. I thought I had to add another person to fill the void that my grandmother left. The truth is God wanted to fill every void. I let my emotions cloud my ability to hear the voice of God and as a result, I missed Him. No matter how many people you surround yourself with, no matter what the people around you tell you. No one can make you whole but GOD! Don't let the enemy fool you into allowing other hurting people into your hurting space. When there is a void in your life, don't fill it with people or things, fill it with God. Trust me, although it may feel good for a while, you will definitely not end up where you want to be (please see Matthew 12:43-45).

Second, everyone that you surround yourself with is a direct reflection of your spiritual state or lack thereof. Some say that people are in your life for a reason or a season. It is my belief that everyone that enters your life adds value to it no matter what length of time you allot them. I like to compare it to a puzzle; God adds pieces and takes pieces away so that we can get a clear picture of what he has in store for our lives. When people come in and go out of our lives we must see if and how they fit. The question then becomes who's putting the puzzle together?

When I was younger, my grandmother used to love putting puzzles together. She would sit at the table in the dining room with pieces scattered all over the place and put the pieces together without looking at the picture on the box. I would sit there and watch her for hours afraid to ask the obvious question. Once I just asked her, "How do you know what you are trying to make?" She said, "I don't, but eventually I will. Knowing the picture does not change the need to put the pieces in the right place." Many of us are going through life so focused on the pieces that we forget that God has the big picture in mind. Instead of allowing him to piece together our lives, we do it ourselves. We force things into our lives that don't fit. We go to church and sing, dance, pray and shout, then come home and hang with people who have no idea what it means or what it costs to live for God. We must grow in boldness in our faith and live it completely. Don't settle for religion, rather get relationship. Be comfortable saying to anyone not seeking God what Joshua said, *"And if it seem evil unto you to serve the LORD, choose you this day whom ye will serve; whether the gods which your fathers served that were on the other side of the flood, or the gods of the Amorites, in whose land ye dwell: but as for me and my house, we will serve the LORD"* (Joshua 24:15).

Third, and because I don't have a better way to put it, "Pride goes before destruction, and a haughty spirit before a fall." (Proverbs 16:18) We all, and I do mean ALL, are flawed people. I typically ask people the question, "If God made you perfect, what would you need him for?" Even Paul fought with this idea for a while until God had to tell him that His grace was all he needed (2 Corinthians 12:7-10). Too many times we fool ourselves (again me included) into thinking we are delivered from something and that we are alright, until we are forced to confront that thing. We have to believe in our deliverance and walk in our deliverance. Stand with God and let Him hide you from every enemy, even when that the enemy is you!

I know that above is a lot to digest, but here are some simple principles to gather from this:

1) Surround yourself with the presence of God. This will ensure that you have every opportunity to enjoy God's freedom from any and everything that binds you. (Psalm 16:11)

2) The only way to dwell in the light of God is to be separated from the darkness of the world. (John 12:46 and Romans 12:2)

3) Tell me who your friends are and I will tell you who you are! Whoever you surround yourself with is a mirror reflection of who you are or will become. (Proverbs 13:20)

4) Trust God's view! All we can see are the trees. The forest is a view that God saved for himself! (Proverbs 3:5, Isaiah 55:8-9)

5) DO NOT be the devil's best weapon! (James 1:13-15)

Have you ever watched an action movie and wondered how on earth the bad guy sometimes loses? I mean, he has the good guy right where he wants him and then all of a sudden everything is turned around. The crazier part is when the bad guy tells the good guy exactly what his plan is, so once free, the good guy knows exactly how to stop him. Just plain buffoonery if you ask me. Well that is the same way sin operates! Unfortunately, we have succumbed to sin in such a manner that we have to constantly struggle with it, but as stated previously the fight we are fighting is in some sense an attempt to do the wrong thing. We attempt to conquer our sin. Stand over it victoriously and subdue it. The truth of scripture is that we are to be overcomers. Now to some that difference is subtle, but there truly is a great divide between the two. A conqueror takes hold of a thing makes it their own and a part of them. When the Roman Empire conquered nations they became an extension of Rome. It would be foolish to make sin a part of you.

We are called to be more than conquerors (Romans 8:37). We are called to be overcomers. The primary difference being an overcomer does away with what it has defeated. You destroy a thing, and you remove yourself from the attachment of the thing. If it is our flesh that is causing us to be led astray from the perfect will and purpose of God, then we must connect to God in such a way that he does away with our desires. You often hear people say that God will give you the "desires of your heart" (Psalms 37.) Most take this to mean that God will literally give you whatever you want if you delight in Him. I was once watching TBN and a woman who was paralyzed from the waist down was telling how she was active in ministry, leading people to God and living for God, and all she wanted from God was to walk again. The desire of her heart seemed simple enough. She just wanted to walk. She finished her testimony by saying that God gave her a revelation that when you delight yourself in God, he literally will give you the desires of your heart. This woman never walked again, but had joy, peace and happiness because when she delighted in God, God changed her desire from a desire to walk to a desire for Him. We overcome sin by trusting the God and Savior who overcame the world. Delight yourself in the Lord, and let him give you the desires of your heart!

No Levels

Finally, and I am not going to belabor this point at all: SIN IS SIN. There are no levels in hell that you go to if you do one sin or another. A liar will be next to a murderer. Separation from the presence of God is just that, and any moment away from his presence is a moment of torture. Although we discuss and debate what is or isn't, the truth is that no amount of discussion can make any sin any worse than another. Jesus conquered death, hell and the grave so the consequence of sin is defeated for the saved. No sin you have or can commit will make God forgive you more or less. Forgiven is forgiven, and "if any man be in Christ he is a new creation" (2 Corinthians 5:17). My grandmother would always say, "Right is right and wrong is wrong." Whatever is accepted by God is accepted by

God, not because we say so but because God says so. The ultimate judge of a man's soul is God. Conviction comes from God, but flows through us to reach others. The moment that we place our opinions on the ordinances of the spirit of God, then we lead people astray. Debating sin does not edify the church, rather overcoming sin, the flesh and the enemy does! Let's stop fighting each other and accept that all have sinned, and all can receive forgiveness.

WHAT'S LOVE GOT TO DO WITH IT: LOVE

Once I was talking to my grandmother about marriage and love. I explained to her the type of woman I wanted to marry, the things I would want from a wife and what I would and would not accept in marriage. In the midst of my rambling, she says to me, "How do you know that you love somebody?" I told her that you know when you know" (as if that makes sense)! She pressed me again and again to define what love is. So I said what I heard someone else say, love is never having to say I'm sorry. I thought that was so deep and profound. She, in turn, replied by asking a series of what if questions. What if your wife cheated, would you leave? What if she cheated with your best friend, would you leave? After a series of yes and no responses I said, "Grandma, love wouldn't allow someone to do all of that." Her reply was simple: "Love may not do all of that, but love will endure all of that." She then asked me, "What is the worst thing that a woman could ever do to you?" I replied to her that the worst thing a woman can do to me is cause me to fear her. Not a fear in terms of her physically hitting me (I am a pretty big guy), but fear of what she is capable of doing to my heart and spirit. She said, "If you can endure that, then you know you truly have love." This was not an suggestion to stick anything out, but rather that a heart willing to endure is a heart that holds love. The difference between "willing to" and "capable of" is great and deserves its own book. But I digress.

Love is complex and yet simple at the same time. The basic premise that you first must understand is that God is Love. In grasping that, you have to take the truth about God and compare it to the things that define love. First Corinthians 13:4-13 says:

"Love is patient, love is kind. It does not envy, it does not boast, it is not proud. It does not dishonor others, it is not self-seeking, it is not easily angered, it keeps no record of wrongs. Love does not delight in evil but rejoices with the truth. It always protects, always trusts, always hopes, always perseveres.

Love never fails. But where there are prophecies, they will cease; where there are tongues, they will be stilled; where there is knowledge, it will pass away. For we know in part and we prophesy in part, but when completeness comes, what is in part disappears. When I was a child, I talked like a child; I thought like a child, I reasoned like a child. When I became a man, I put the ways of childhood behind me. For now we see only a reflection as in a mirror; then we shall see face to face. Now I know in part; then I shall know fully, even as I am fully known.

And now these three remain: faith, hope and love. But the greatest of these is love."

Often we look at these scriptures as just being some simple explanation of love. To be honest, I have used them for good and for not so good reasons. Love can apply to so many things and so many situations, but with that being said let's start from the beginning. As with anything there are two types of love: the world view and the faith or God view. Love, according to the world, is an expression of deep feelings that accompany certain traits and actions. This love is defined by the finite. What that means is there is a beginning to it and inevitably there is an end. Let me explain. Typically people say that they must find someone to love, but the truth is that love is not something to find but something to be revealed. The world looks for love, while the believer has a revelation that love is there (remember God is Love).

So to further explore this notion of the world's love vs. God's love we have to also identify how it is expressed. The world's love speaks to something that is pleasing and appealing to the senses. For example, a guy and a girl are dating, and he does everything that the girl could even think or dream of wanting. They take trips, he buys gifts, he always says what she wants to hear and is always encouraging. He wears the right cologne, can cook and fills her every thought. When the girl is questioned about love, she talks about all the things he does, all the things he says and all the ways he makes her happy. He never makes her feel pain and never makes her question herself, but makes her feel comfortable. This type of love sounds good but is not good for you. Her reasons for loving him are based on tangible things of the world that appeal to the things of the world.

The bible says in 1 John 2:16, "*For all that is in the world, the lust of the flesh and the lust of the eyes and the boastful pride of life, is not from the Father, but is from the world.*" I know this may seem irrelevant, but take a closer look at the guy and girl scenario. The girl loves how the guy looks and smells and he appears to be doing all the superficial things that a person would say is love. She sees these things in movies, in the books and possibly in the relationships around her and she takes that to be what love is. When the truth is that it is possibly only the appearance of love (LUST OF THE EYES). Then she talks about the way she feels and how her emotions are uncontrollable and that he, a man she is not married to, has control of her heart. She speaks of how their kiss is just right and when they are intimate his love is "the best." He makes her feel good (LUST OF THE FLESH), and beyond all of that he never makes her feel challenged or crazy for making some of her decisions. He makes her feel great about where she is and says if she never changes that would be great, and beyond that they look good together. She believes that she deserves a person like that. She has suffered through so much mess she earned this good man (PRIDE OF LIFE).

Worldly love comes from two places: a feeling of longing and a sense of entitlement. This kind of love takes the pleasurable nature of a relationship (whether it is friendship, romantic, familial or otherwise) and defines that as what love is or should be. Unfortunately, that sentiment has crept its way into the church. Love should only be expressed in an acceptable manner, to acceptable people. Love has come to be expressed through the gospel of Janet Jackson which asks, "What have you done for me lately?" A great example of worldly love is expressed through Leah in Genesis 29:32. In this scripture, Leah believes it is her ability to do something that Rachel could not that would cause Jacob to love her. Today we make people feel like if they cannot be of use in the church then they are not deserving of our love. Sadly, just like Jacob, even after people do what is needed in the church, they still, for one reason or another, are not recipients of the love of the church. We dismiss this notion by saying, we can love them and still be cautious about them, or we can love them and still harbor feelings about their former sins. What if

God's relationship with the church were the same way the church's relationship is with the people of God? God's love is one of the many missions of the church. If we are not spreading the love of God, then we are spreading the love of the world.

Now, Godly love can be described by many words. Sometimes we talk about *agape, eros* or *phileo*; all of the Greek words used to describe what love is and the nature of love. Simply put, Godly love is one word: unconditional. The point that my grandmother wanted me to see was not necessarily all the stuff I should deal with in a relationship, but rather the type of things that love will allow me to endure, regardless of the source. Whether it's in a friendship, a family or a marriage, love endures the hard times and appreciates the good times. God requires believers to love our enemies (Matthew 5:43-48 or Luke 6:27-36). Correction has its place, only if the motive for correction is love and protection.

Now with this thought in mind, the idea that love is about protection, take a peek through the bible and read the stories of Job, or Jonah, or Moses, or David and Uriah, or Joseph, or how about Jesus. Every one of those stories will make you ask the question, "How is God protecting them?" He allowed so much to happen to them, and yet he loved them. This is what will make most people who are struggling with belief ask the all-important question, "What's love got to do with that?" Instead of going on and on about the plan of God, the love of God and the righteousness of God which may serve to further confuse the point, what we all need to understand is that it all works together.

A farmer would hate a life with only sunshine, just as much as he would hate a life with only rain. God uses trials and tribulations to prepare us to do more in our next level of growth to mature us in wisdom and power. James 1 declares that we should be happy when we are going through trials as it is a sign that God is grooming us for more growth. God promises tribulation and he promises persecution, but through it all he promises *"all things work together for the good of them who love Him and are called according to his purpose."* He promises that he loved us so much that if we believe in him that we will have everlasting life with Him, not in the world.

Now let's make this practical for the skeptic. Love looks at the heart of a person through discernment, and judges them accordingly. We do not alienate those who have made mistakes because the truth according to scripture is that all have sinned and fallen short of the glory of God! But in our failings, Paul in Romans 8:35-39 reminds us *"nothing can separate us from the love of God!"* Love is not a warm, fuzzy feeling, but as discussed previously love requires a sacrifice, from the person who gives and from the person who receives it. Simply put God's love changes people, while worldly love just changes!

THE GOOD LIFE: SALVATION

Most people when you ask them about salvation three things particularly come into mind. First is the cross, since the foundation of our faith stands on the "finished work" of the cross. The cross represents the shedding of the old man, the crucified flesh, the blood (got to have the blood) and the greatest sacrifice that any man has known, the sacrifice of life for a friend (John 15:13). It represents the opening of the gateway that was closed and the reconciliation of the creator and his creation. For more reasons than can be expressed in this book, typically the first thought that comes to most people's mind is simply the "passion of Christ."

The second thing that tends to come to mind after the cross is grace. The bible even declares that we are saved by grace through faith, not of ourselves but as a gift from God (Ephesians 2:8). Grace is what covers us and keeps us, and it is grace that provides protection. Grace is like an eraser. When I was a kid my mom hated when I would do my homework with a pen. While she would usually let it slide with most subjects, she refused to let me use a pen for my math homework. It would bother me to my core when she wouldn't let me use a pen, because I figured if I were writing it then I was sure of the answer. Beyond that pencils would break, get lost and sometimes they would not even have an eraser. Also, since pens were always readily available in my house so I just used pens. Once I was using a pen to do my math, since it was before my mother got home. I worked on the problems, filled in the answers and was finished.

When my mother came home she asked if my homework done, and of course I said yes. She asked to see it, so I showed her. When looking over my math homework, she started to have a funny look on her face. She noticed that I had missed a problem, and as a result all of my answers were off. She reached for a pencil to erase the answers, but I had to tell her that I used a pen. She then said if I had used a pencil I would not have to do it all over again because I could just erase the wrong answers and fix them. God looks at our life and decisions as written in pencil.

When we make a mistake, God does not start us from the beginning of our journey, but rather at the point of our mistake. Grace allows God to say "all things work together for the good of them that love Him and are called according to his purpose" (Romans 8:28). Grace says that God will take our good and our bad and weigh them against our heart and his purpose and judge us, not because of what we deserve, but based on his love for us. Salvation, to some, represents the greatest "eraser" in our lives, which means the greatest display of God's grace.

But whether you think of the cross or grace, everyone, when they think of salvation, immediately thinks of this third thing: Romans 10:9. I know people that have never set foot in a church and know that scripture almost better than some people who are in church every Sunday. For those who have not read it, Romans 10:9 says, "If you declare with your mouth Jesus is Lord and believe in your heart that God raised him from the dead, you will be saved." Essentially, the proposition of salvation seems simple enough: a confession and a belief. Sunday after Sunday, every church in America and possibly the world gives people the opportunity to make the confession of faith and say they believe both propositions: that Jesus is Lord and God raised him from the dead. Often it is in conjunction with the "opening of the church doors" by inviting new believers to become members of the church. Week after week, hundreds of thousands of people make these confessions and truly believe that they are saved. But what if there is more to obtaining salvation than reciting this scripture or prayer? Now before I go any further, let me be clear. Christ gives salvation, and it is free!!! The requirement of salvation is clearly stated biblically in Romans 10:9. I am not attempting to make anyone think that anything you "do" can make you any more saved than the next person. However, let's try and fully understand what this scripture is telling us as it relates to the two principles that are paramount in this chapter: confession and belief.

Confession

Within the last decade or so, the church went into a cycle that I like to call the "name it and claim it" phase. Essentially what this says is that what we say is ours will be ours. Want a new car? Name it and claim it! Want a new house? Name it and claim it! Want more than enough? Name it and claim it! While this idea has some truth, I believe it is fundamentally flawed. Jesus repeated throughout scripture what I have learned to be the A.S.K. principle: *"ask and you shall have, seek and you shall find, knock and the door will be opened."* (Matthew 7:7) Now this sounds very easy, but to simply think about it in the name it and claim it manner would be to relegate God to a genie. Not a sovereign God, but a deity that is subject to a sovereign people. If this is the case, then confession would be nothing more than just speaking out of want.

James gives us a clearer understanding about the things that we ask of God. In Chapter 4, he says, *"You desire, but you do not have, so you kill. You covet, but you cannot get what you want, so you quarrel and fight. You do not have because you do not ask God. When you ask, you do not receive because you ask with wrong motives that you may spend what you get on your pleasures."* James wants us to see that it is our motives that determine what we are able to receive from God. Asking is half the battle, but at the heart of it all understanding that why you are asking is directly connected to what you receive from God. Why you ask separates a statement from a confession.

There is a big difference between what we say and what we confess. A person can speak mindlessly. If I say the sky is purple, I can say it and leave it at that but that doesn't make it true. Now I really don't think I would say the sky is purple unless I was inebriated, on some type of hallucinogenic or some spirits that didn't come from God. The point is, empty words carry no weight with the listener. The word "confess" in our scripture in Romans, literally breaks down to two words in the Greek which mean together (*homo*) and "of speech" (*logos*). What this means is that what you speak must come from the agreement of your mind, heart and spirit and be conveyed through your words. When God created everything, the

Father, Son and Spirit were as one and on one accord. Proof of this is that as he made man he stated, "let us make man in our image" (Genesis 1:26). For a confession to be made, we must get to a place where our mind, heart and the Spirit of God in us are aligned, and we act on that confession. Our confessions of faith manifest when every part of our being is in alignment with everything that God is. So in this way, what we say is only as great as what we believe.

Belief

One of the most interesting times in recent history was December of 1999. There was a widespread belief in that year that bringing in the New Year meant bringing in the destruction of the world, or as it was called, Y2K. For many people around the world, they truly believed that the world was going to end, and as a result of this belief they began to stock up on non-perishable foods and water to be prepared. Those that knew about this but did not believe did little if anything to prepare. What you believed would happen after December 31, 1999 at 11:59:59 determined exactly what and how you lived in the days, weeks and months that preceded it. In this same way, belief cannot and is not something that we simply hold on to but rather something we live out. It's easy to dismiss David Koresh or the many other people that declared the end of the world, but the truth is what they believed defined how they lived.

Belief, as stated previously, is the foundation of our faith. What is interesting about the relationship between salvation and belief is what it is that we are called to believe to be saved. Using our foundational scripture (Romans 10:9), we are called to *"Believe in your heart that God raised him from the dead."* Now that seems like an interesting proposition on its own, but let's look further to see what Paul says about this belief. In the next verse he says, *"For it is with your heart that you believe and are justified..."* But what does it mean to believe with your heart and what exactly do we have to believe?

The conjoined twin of belief is faith, as it relates to the development of a believer and Christian. Faith requires a belief in the existence of God and the reward of diligence in seeking him (Hebrews 11:6). So to be grounded in your faith you must be willing to pursue what you believe although you cannot see what you believe. Taking it a step further, belief requires that you respond to it through corresponding action. It is impossible to believe something to be true in your heart and not act accordingly. A person that believes that she is supposed to be an artist does everything in her power to become an artist. A person who believes he can get a college degree pursues the degree until he has attained it. Belief, as mentioned, means to be completely convinced. Standing on a belief can be difficult because standing on a belief means you are not necessarily standing on or grounded by facts. A child believes in Santa Claus and his ability to go to every house in the world and deliver toys to all of the good children. Conversely, when that child subsequently sees their groggy parents struggling to put together a bike or put presents under the tree, the belief is trumped by what they now know.

Now look at what the scripture declares we must believe again, but in the greater context. Romans says God raised Jesus from the dead, but why is this proclamation that Paul makes the foundation of our belief unto salvation? Why is our salvation contingent on this belief? What if I told you that your salvation was contingent on truth and possibilities? In a previous chapter, I mentioned that the word of God is infallible truth. The greatest truth revealed in the word is the manifestation of God's word of truth, through the person, life, death and resurrection of Christ. It is here that we find the intersection of what we are called to believe. Belief in the resurrection of Christ is perhaps the most complicated thing to discuss with people of different faiths, and sometimes people of the same faith, but in essence it is this truth that we find as our solid foundation for the relevancy of God, Jesus and the word.

If we are unable to open ourselves up to the prophetic revelation of the meaning behind the resurrection of Christ, then it is at this point of departure that we can throw away the rest of the book. If God cannot raise Jesus (who is a part of Himself) from the dead, then all possibilities of whom God is ends there. If we can and do believe this fact, then we become open to understanding how great God is and can be in our lives. God can only be what we believe him to be, and at the end of it all the great reward that awaits the diligent seeker is salvation. If salvation is not possible, then we are all living pointlessly!

Now how does the belief about salvation differ between the word and the current church? The church believes that the confession creates salvation. It believes that a confession of your beliefs means that you believe what you confessed. From the perspective of the word, confession cannot precede belief. In that sense, a confession has to be rooted, planted and grounded by a belief. Before you can make a confession of salvation you must first believe that salvation is possible. Knowing scripture, reciting scripture and church membership are not prerequisites to salvation. Instead it is a belief in the possibilities of an omnipotent God to the point where you believe that he can give you salvation.

So the question becomes how can we go from a confession of faith to a confession from faith? The first step is to understand that emotion cannot drive a decision to be saved. There is a stark difference between being moved by a minister and being moved by the Spirit of God. It requires that you come to the church in search of God and not in search of a great word, a great choir, or nice "churchy people." Emotions can cloud our judgment and remove us from being receptive to a revelation of God. Take emotion out of the confession and belief and allow it to be driven by you becoming "persuaded" by the spirit of God. Now before going any further, please understand that the same can be said for overly logical people, like me. Salvation is not something you can reason your way into, as our logic will only leave us with a list of somewhat unanswerable questions. Logic, like emotions, places the emphasis on why we need God now, but the spirit of God leads us to the conclusion that we always needed God. Making a logical or emotional decision to be saved can only last as long as that feeling or reasoning is pertinent to you.

Second, after we have been persuaded we must accept the responsibility to act on what we have now chosen to believe. Our belief must not end at salvation, just as our Christianity does not end with a Romans 10:9 confession. If faith without works is dead, and our salvation is based on a confession of faith (Romans 10:10), then I suggest that salvation without works is also dead. Proof of salvation does not come in a bible-toting, "blessed and highly favored" shouting form. Rather, proof of salvation comes by way of converting your faith into something tangible. If people not moved beyond writing a check, visiting a church, crying on the slow songs, shouting on the fast songs and telling everyone that comes to them with an issue, "I'll pray for you" then it is my belief that they may need to reevaluate their salvation.

Which leads me to my last point which is extremely redundant, but God gives salvation as a gift and you cannot earn salvation. As the scripture says, we are saved by grace through faith. Salvation is the substance of our hope and the evidence of our unseen belief. While I hold fast to the fact that salvation, as with all things of God, produces evidence and manifests in some way, it is the spirit that moves us to act on that belief. It is not our misguided want only to be accepted by God but a faith-filled confession that we are accepted by God. Simply put, salvation is God's gift to give, and it is our responsibility to get into a position to receive it.

I once saw a friend drowning, not figuratively but literally. At this time, I was not a good enough swimmer to go get him out of the water, so I went and got a lifeguard. The lifeguard dives into the water, gets to him and attempts to pull him out, but he would not stop flailing his arms all over the place. As a result, the lifeguard could not get hold of him. After about five minutes of fighting in the water, the lifeguard punched my friend in the side such that his arms immediately collapsed to his side. At this point, the lifeguard grabbed hold of him and pulled him out of the water. Now I am sure that may not have been perfect protocol, but when my friend asked him why he hit him, the lifeguard said, "If I didn't hit you, you wouldn't have let me save you." Sometimes our fear can place us in a position where our heart is flailing around searching for a way to stay afloat. We attempt to save ourselves from sin, trials and tribulation, and all can serve as a sea of despair. What we need to understand is that God will do whatever he needs to do to get us to a place where we can be saved, even if he has to hurt us to save us. Believe that God can save you, then let him do it.

The church has become like I was. We are close enough to those who are drowning, but unequipped to pull them out ourselves. It is an awesome thing to be able to go to God so he can do what we cannot, but it is even greater to know that our salvation and faith can mature us to a place where we desire to share and save everyone we see drowning. Belief to faith, faith to confession, confession to salvation; let this be the driving order that takes our salvation from being what we say to being what we live!

LIFE AFTER THE BENEDICTION

A few weeks after my encounter with the man in the barber shop in the first chapter, I actually ran into him again, literally. I was walking toward the shop while using my cell phone and ran into him, but I digress. Before I went into the shop, I asked him how everything was going and how his family had been. He began to tell me that he started visiting churches with his family and was trying to find a place he could call his church home. He said that the search was going well and the family was enjoying it, especially his wife. I gave him brotherly congrats and prepared to go into the shop. As I walked toward the door he said, "What now though?" Not clear what he meant, I turned and asked him. He said, "I enjoy going to church and cannot wait to find a place to go every Sunday. My kids have started to pick out stuff they want to do in the church, and so have my wife and I, but what about life. I still have to live after church." Without telling all of his story, he proceeded to tell me that several unfortunate things had happened to his family and that the church helps them take their minds off of it while they are there, but it has done nothing to help him deal with his problems.

Too often we face the same dilemma and are never as candid or willing to say it to anyone in the church. The truth in life is that Christians are fired and hired at the same rate as the rest of the world. Christians are not exempt from foreclosure, divorce, murder, or any other tragedy of life. So what makes life after the service different than life before it began? Fundamentally, you would presume that everything you need to live after service is given to you during the service. This is just not true. The easy explanation would be my favorite phrase to start any conversation, "It depends," but that leaves too many possibilities. So what is the answer? Where can we find the truth of what this walk is all about? Very simply you can find it in God. Now that may seem like a daunting task given how great God is and how many ways he is defined – just in this book, and the many ways I invariably missed. So what does that mean? It means to just live a B.A.D. Life: Balanced and Disciplined Life. The intent of the church should be to give Christians the principles of God as lived through the example of Christ. Christ's life exemplified what it meant to be balanced and disciplined, two very important factors of our Christian walk that will leave very little misunderstood.

Balance

Growing up, I got the distinct impression that my mother and grandparents did not like me. Don't get me wrong, I knew they loved me (most of the time at least), but I really began to think that they truly did not like me. I figured this out every other night at the dinner table. They would load up my plate every night with all the tasty stuff I like, and then all of a sudden they would throw something green and funny-looking on my plate. As I got older, this truth became even more prevalent as I started to go to my friend's birthday parties. I would get there facing a smorgasbord of delectable treats (I needed to use a big word to explain the big smile that covered my face). I would go there and eat cake, pizza, fried chicken and french fries; I was living the dream! Then I would walk out of the door and get a "goodie bag" of more treats and candy. Now the fact that I would be up all that night with a stomach ache didn't matter to me; all that mattered was that everything I wanted, I had.

Unfortunately, the church has become oversized versions of me as a kid. We go to churches that seek to cater to what we want at the cost of not wanting to be fed what we need. Most of the concepts you have read in this book play themselves out in that battle. We have become so afraid of losing members that we never build Christians. Pastors have become paid caterers and not loving parents. Instead of feeding us what we need and dealing with our tantrums, they lay out all the things we like in a way that will appeal to us and allow us to take what we want and leave what we don't. The mandate that Christ put on Peter was that if he loved him, to "feed my sheep."

We have moved into a place where we believe catering serves the purpose of feeding. A caterer is always pleasing the people and getting paid for it because it is their job. A parent's concern is the health and growth of the child. A healthy diet is defined by one very simple word: BALANCE.

Life, both in the natural and in the spirit, requires a balance. Ecclesiastes 3 tells us that there is a time for everything. As much as we require being encouraged, we need just as much, if not more, to be corrected. In Hebrews 12:5-6 Paul says, "Have you completely forgotten this word of encouragement that addresses you as a father addresses his son? My son, do not make light of the Lord's discipline, and do not lose heart when he rebukes you, because the Lord disciplines the one he loves and he chastens everyone he accepts as a son." The love of God requires His correction to those that go astray from time to time. An uncorrected child loses focus. A child with no focus has no vision, and where there is no vision, a people perish (cast off restraint) (Proverbs 29:18). A part of living beyond the four walls of the sanctuary requires an understanding that balance does not mean you hit the club as much as you hit the church. Balance says that I live according to God's ordinances and I trust His righteous judgment not only when I am good, but when I am not.

Balance also speaks to how we make our decisions. Balance weighs the true value of a thing against its counterpart, but does so equally. What does this mean? The bible says that, "a false balance is an abomination…" (Proverbs 11:1). How we make our decisions goes beyond just a simple WWJD (for those of you that missed this phenomenon, WWJD means What Would Jesus Do, and congrats for crawling from under that rock!). The idea that we will make a decision as Jesus did does not speak to the ability to gauge how Jesus decided what he would do. Christ understood that the eternal always trumps the temporary. Why settle for what you can have physically, which is limited when you can have something spiritual that can manifest in more than one way? Balance places this life into perspective. Christ understood this fact, as proven through his temptation in the wilderness. He was offered everything, except what could last. When making balanced decisions, you must weigh as Christ did the flesh against the spirit; what is eternal versus what is temporal.

Discipline

There is more we can learn from the temptation of Christ than has been mentioned. Every time the devil offers him something, he replies with an "It is written…" Most would take that as simply Jesus knowing scripture, but another part of that is him being disciplined enough to sit and learn scripture. We take for granted the human nature of Jesus and, as such, we make presumptions about what he did and did not have to deal with. For example, Luke 2:46-52 gives a different view of Christ. Some may believe that Jesus needed to be spanked for running away, which is what my mom would have done if I told her that I was about my father's business, but that is neither here nor there. What you find here is a Jesus eager to learn more and understand more. What you see here as well is the results of his discipline in verse 52 as it states, "Jesus grew in wisdom and stature and in favor with God and man."

A huge struggle of the church is that we believe that because we are growing we can forfeit the process of discipline. I have a teenage brother who is now and will continue to grow taller than me. Yes, I have dealt with this fact through prayer and fasting. *Since he was a kid*, I would teach him how to play basketball. When I went to the park to play, he followed. Eventually, he wanted to learn more about the game and so he shadowed me. Every once in a while he would try and play against me, and every time he played better and better. There was one occasion where he was working really hard at his game. At the end of his practicing, he tried to play me one-on-one. Of course I said yes and he starts playing, and for the first part of the game I keep it close, then he wins. He starts yelling and getting all excited and just because I am a mean big brother, I told him the truth: I let him win. He swore up and down that he won fair and square and that he was ready to prove it right then and there. So, we played again. Without giving a specific score, please just know that he lost REALLY BADLY! After the game, I told him that while he was good, skill will never be equal to experience and discipline.

Robert Charles Sproul, American Calvinist theologian, author, and pastor wrote in one of his books, In Search of Dignity, "The church is called not only to a ministry of reconciliation, but a ministry of nurture to those within her gates. Part of that nurture includes church discipline." Today we are too willing to substitute talent for pure discipline. Talent can get you noticed, discipline is what sustains you. A part of successfully living the Christian walk requires discipline. Without discipline, the church cannot move in power. Discipline in the word and discipline in the community of believers is what allows us to not only grow, but to grow together. Discipline takes the course of our lives and regardless of trials, test or temptations it pushes you to stay that course. Discipline is in line and directly connected to obedience, but it takes obedience a step further. Discipline is consistent obedience. It is in our discipline that we find ourselves connected to the purpose and plan of God. The "great commission" of God required that the church go and "make disciples of men." When the church ceases to make disciples and it only recruits members, it is a church that has failed to see the true meaning of building Christians. One last thing to note. Christ being our ultimate example exhibited a life of discipline; one that adheres to the movement and the discernment of the Spirit of God. So, before we were ever shown how to sacrifice, we were taught how to be disciplined.

As for the man outside the barber shop, I could have told him a million things. I could have told him to just do it, like the church and Nike says. After I took a minute, I told him this story: There was once a man on a road trip. While he was on his road trip, he was using the brand new GPS his wife had just bought him. He did not know how to use it very well, nor did he fully understand how it worked, all he knew was that if he put in a destination the device would show him how to get there, step-by-step. So he gets in the car, enters the address and begins his journey. At one point during the trip he stops for gas and cleans out some of the things in his car. When cleaning out the car, he unintentionally touches the language change screen on his GPS, making the voice and words on the GPS now in a language he could not understand. He gets in his car and in a slight panic simply begins to drive down the road he was previously on heading in the direction he previously was heading. While driving and trying to ignore the voice and the words from the GPS, he sees there is a highlighted line showing him his path. Also, it has a dot that shows him exactly where he is. He begins to follow the path, turning as the dot needs to stay on the path. Eventually he reaches his destination.

Sometimes when we are heading toward God, it almost feels as though His people are changing the language of the signs pointing to

Him. When we go to the scriptures we have the sermon of the preacher in our heads, and so the words of God take on what we have heard, which may have value, but is not what we see in the scripture. God's word is more than just a word, but it is a "Lamp to my feet and a light to my path."(Psalm 119:105) God's revelation can find you no matter where you are in your walk. God can move us to where he needs us to be. The church is a place where we can find out what and who God is and can set us on our great path toward the wonder that is the life of a Christian. Sometimes our best intentions in the church get wrapped up in the monotony that can develop not just in us as individuals, but the church as a whole.

So my advice to him is my advice to you. Follow Christ through the church. Not the church that grants a pass to some sins and condemns you to hell for others. Not the church that passes empty shouting as praise and emotional tears as worship. Not the church that supports religious agendas and hatred. Not the church that allows for carnal comfort, but HIS CHURCH! The church that he said, "the gates of Hell could not prevail against," in Matthew 16:18. Many things can become difficult and confusing, but as long as we follow the way, the truth and the life, we never have to worry about being lost in church translation, but can rejoice by being found in church relationship with Christ.

ACKNOWLEDGMENTS

There are a number of people that influenced me and it would literally take an entire book to acknowledge them all. So if you are not mentioned in these acknowledgments, know that you are not forgotten, but I wanted to specifically recognize the people who have affected not just me, but this book in particular. Also, I have to save some names for the second book!

This book does not exist without those who pushed me into ministry and helped me uncover my passion for the gospel. That begins with the two churches that shaped my youth, New Friendship Missionary Baptist Church and New Second Hope Missionary Baptist Church, and the Pastors of those churches, Rev. Dr. Edwin Simmons and Rev. Harold Freeman, and I can't forget my first "First Lady" Delores Freeman. Thank you all for teaching me not to just love God, but the church as well. Also to my god-parents, Apostles David and Linda Patton, thank you for encouraging me to continue to look for God.

To Rev. Dr. Trunell and Rev. Dr. Alexis Felder and New Faith Baptist Church International, thank you for teaching me what boundless ministry truly means. To my New Faith youth, young adults and singles thank you for allowing me to be a part of your journey.

To Rev. Marvin E. Wiley and Rock of Ages Baptist Church, you, sir, are a preaching savant, thank you for opening your doors and life to me. Thank you for all that you allowed me to learn from you.

To the preachers that made me the preacher that I am and try to become daily: Rev. Dr. Frank A. Thomas, who taught me to love the process of preaching and to be dedicated to the work; Rev. Dr. Eugene Gibson, who taught me to be comfortable with myself in the process and to always stretch myself to be better and do more; and Rev. Dr. Paul Sadler, who taught me to be free in the pulpit. To the preachers who I tried to be my best version of early on and who now I continue to admire, Rev. Dr. Jeremiah Wright, Rev. Dr. John Bryant, Rev. Dr. Jamal Bryant, Rev. Dr. Marcus D. Cosby, Rev. Dr. F. Bruce Williams and Rev. Dr. Frederick D. Haynes, III, thank you all for making me realize that the word you deliver is only as impactful to others as the Word that impacts you.

To my teachers and peers at McCormick Theological Seminary,

specifically, Rev. Dr. Joanne Lindstrom, who added to this work's completion, thank you for pushing me to be more introspective in life and ministry, no matter how intimidating that journey may be. Your words changed how I do ministry. To Dr. Reggie Williams, Dr. David Daniels and Dr. Ken Sawyer, who all made me stretch the limits of where the gospel could go and how it could get there. The faith and all theological study is enhanced because of your work. And to Rev. David Watkins, who has always allowed me to vent my; thank you for questioning me at every turn, reminding me that there is often more value in the right question, than a timely answer.

To a few of my brothers in ministry, Rev. Troy Underwood, Min. Ivan Kennedy, Min. Brandon Gatson and Rev. Darryl Scarbrough; if not for your guidance, prayers, encouragement and correction, I would have given up on myself and ministry a long time ago. I honor you and thank God for the blessing you are to my life and ministry.

To my ministry partners and friends, both past and present, thank you all for pushing to be better. I have known many failures and successes in ministry but learned the truth of the Frederick Douglass quote from our work together, "If there is no struggle, there is no progress."

To Covenant U.C.C., thank you for embracing me. To Rev. Rhoda Barnes, thank you for providing guidance during my transition. To the ministerial staff, thank you all for welcoming me. Though I am still learning, I am not sure if I would be where I am if not for all of your guidance along the way; as well as the loving prayers of my brothers in bonds, and sisters in service at Covenant.

Finally, to MY PASTOR, who pushed me to release this work and added to its completion, Rev. Dr. Ozzie E. Smith, Jr. When I came to Covenant, I was in a weird space of deciding if I wanted to continue ministry after seminary. Sitting and watching you during my internship made me realize that it is possible to love the people of God and still care for myself. Thank you for your investment in me and the Covenant I came to know and love. You have created an environment that allows people to find God and themselves and I am grateful for your guidance and support. You are the type of pastor and man that I aspire to be.

www.ingramcontent.com/pod-product-compliance
Lightning Source LLC
Chambersburg PA
CBHW071007160426
43193CB00012B/1961